Twirling

My Kaleidoscope

Shannon Love

The opinions expressed in this manuscript are solely the opinions of the author and do not represent the opinions or thoughts of the publisher. The author has represented and warranted full ownership and/or legal right to publish all the materials in this book.

Twisting My Kaleidoscope
All Rights Reserved.
Copyright © 2015 Shannon Love
v2.0

Cover Photo © 2015 Shannon Love. All rights reserved - used with permission.

This book may not be reproduced, transmitted, or stored in whole or in part by any means, including graphic, electronic, or mechanical without the express written consent of the publisher except in the case of brief quotations embodied in critical articles and reviews.

Outskirts Press, Inc.
http://www.outskirtspress.com

ISBN: 978-1-4787-5550-0

Library of Congress Control Number: 2015905002

Outskirts Press and the "OP" logo are trademarks belonging to Outskirts Press, Inc.

PRINTED IN THE UNITED STATES OF AMERICA

Acknowledgments

Although I enjoy the writing process so much that I tend to become overly absorbed in it, I have never actually written a book. Neither have I enrolled in professional courses—leaving me with a lot to learn. In the nick of time and by happy chance, I found Carol Gaskin, my editor. She not only helped me to revise my project, Carol guided me in ways to expand and develop my memoir with tact and sensitivity. I simply could not have offered the quality of material I have without her top-notch advice.

Nyanidoc from Editor World helped me refine my work even more. With a Ph.D. in behavioral psychology, she has not only mastered the intricacies of good writing, Nyanidoc also understands psychosis on a more proficient level than myself.

Which leads me to the telling of my story. I had the auspicious problem of astounding support—so much so that, for the sake of not overwhelming you, it became necessary to leave out some awesome individuals who contributed immensely to my recovery. One such group was my husband's family. My mother-in-law, brothers-in-law, and sisters-in-law, all responded with love and concern, even when I treated a man they dearly cared for like a monster.

Then there's the three weeks of recuperation we spent with his sister's family in Hawaii—an entire chapter I left out. Her natural nurturing nature, combined with her husband and children's lighthearted outlook, awarded us the perfect environment and companionship we needed to heal.

And my friends! My wonderful, wonderful friends! Incorporating scenes with all of them would likely throw your own mind into a state of confusion. Thus I had to choose three. That being said, some of the others might find their words spoken through the mouths of the chosen ones. Shall I ramble off a few names from Houston? Alexa, Grant, Kate, Toni, Craig, Tracey, Mariana, Roger, Joachim, Karin, Mark, Pat, Sondra, Patrick, Macy, Eithne, Erik, Chio Yin, and Jackson, thank you! But the first group to rush to my aid were the Beijingers: Leila, Thomas, Shannon, Marc, Jocelyn, Nick, Ching, Matt, Marieke, Thijs, Sheedvash, Leann, Tony, Lea, Shai, Gloria, Buffy, Steve, Catherine, Kevin, Lauren, Mike, Evelyn, Bill, Birgett, Allister, Mr. Li, Tien Ju Hong—and so many more!

Then, at the last minute, two old friends of mine that I had not seen in years came to my rescue. I needed a couple of very intelligent people, who knew nothing about my psychotic breaks to read the story. Before submitting my work to a publisher, I had to know if my book conveyed itself clearly and could hold the reader's attention. Michelle and Meredith stepped up to the plate.

Do you recall the number of professionals assisting me? I cannot complain about any of them. They were all excellent and it was their unique styles combined that provided the repertoire of skills I acquired. That being said, a few stood out as exceptional. Those being: Dr. Joanne Parham, Dr. DanVy Mui, Aram Sohigian, Dr. George Hu, and Dennis Malloy.

And then came more—my parents, brothers, sisters-in-law, aunts, uncles, and cousins. Every one of them encouraged me, even during my darkest hour. Their calls, cards, and visits to the hospital demonstrated a loyalty that even madness cannot penetrate. They also wrapped their arms around my husband and children during this tumultuous event. But I want to extend my most gracious gratitude to my mom and dad. No one could have possibly given more of themselves both physically and emotionally than they did. They even accompanied us to Hawaii.

All parents brag on their amazing children, for our offspring is our legacy. If we're lucky—they are a better form of us—or even some extraordinary combination of recessive genes, bolstered by environment. I'm one of the fortunate ones. All three of my kids are truly amazing. Not only did they survive the unthinkable—Mom losing her mind, they grew from it, becoming more empathetic individuals than many adults. I've lectured them perpetually over the years to not judge others. "You don't know the story behind an individual's feelings, beliefs, and behaviors," I would say. They listened.

But the gold medal goes to my husband. Uncomfortable in the spotlight, I will honor his wishes of continuing with his fictitious name, Charles. Nevertheless, he can't help but shine. During my sickness, I put this magnanimous man through hell. In return, he taught me about unconditional love. Although we tend to expect this from our parents—possibly even our children; our spouses generally have limits. There is a line that, if crossed, usually leads to divorce. I audaciously crossed that line. That's when Charles loved me enough for the two of us. And that's why I dedicate this book to him.

Understanding that a knight in shining armor might be considered outdated, I say not so. If we understand that the one sitting upon the horse can either be male or female, we more liberal souls might better be able to accept the cliche. Since I was the one in harm's way, my hero happened to be my soul-mate—the most beautiful man in the world.

I love you without end, baby! Never let me forget it.

I dedicate this book to my husband. For, together, we persevered.

Table of Contents

Chapter One: Genesis 1
Chapter Two: Fidgeting..17
Chapter Three: Offering...39
Chapter Four: Obstacles...47
Chapter Five: Upside-Down Cake................................63
Chapter Six: Patience 73
Chapter Seven: Uncommon Senses 89
Chapter Eight: Amazing Grace.....................................99
Chapter Nine: Release 119
Chapter Ten: Adieux 127
Chapter Eleven: Doors...141
Chapter Twelve: Encore...155
Chapter Thirteen: Optimism 163
Chapter Fourteen: Remorse.......................................173
Chapter Fifteen: Dismay 181
Chapter Sixteen: Destiny? 191
Chapter Seventeen: Rodeos 199
Chapter Eighteen: My Tablet.....................................205
Chapter Nineteen: Sorcery 213
Chapter Twenty: Concession 221
Chapter Twenty-one: Accountability 227

Chapter Twenty-two: Despair...239
Chapter Twenty-three: Stratagem 243
Chapter Twenty-four: Evidence..255
Chapter Twenty-five: Emerald City 265
Note From Author 283
Epilogue...287
Disclaimer..289

Introduction

Although I am no expert in psychology, I am a master of my own story: a journey from sanity to lunacy and back again. If you are up for this expedition, I will paint you into the consciousness of the psychotic—transiting you through my experiences, an existence foreign to the mentally sound. My thoughts will divulge the rationale behind such outlandish behavior. My eyes will unmask taboo symptoms that torment the afflicted. And my heart will bear witness to the distress psychosis renders.

Possibly, in the end, you may even be able to relate. Empowered with knowledge, a sense of empathy might allow you to connect with the mentally deranged. Instead of an unhinged lunatic you may glimpse the punctured soul—a mere human being like you, who has been taken from her safe place and positioned in another world, filled with delusions and hallucinations.

Why should you care? Because approximately one in a hundred people suffer from psychosis. If your social circle extends to that number then, most likely, someone you know and care about lives with this disorder. And although the stigma attached to those plagued by this syndrome prevents many from sharing, they wish they could. So in their honor, I will.

I now offer my gift to you: a peek through my kaleidoscope.

Chapter One:

Genesis

"**EVERYTHING LOOKS GOOD,** Mrs. Love. You're almost finished. We just need an ECG reading and you may go home."

Speaking words I longed to hear, the nurse led me to my final test. Avant-Garde Alloy Services (AGAS), my husband's employer, required an annual physical for its expats. It was their way of ensuring that our healthcare needs did not extend beyond the medical resources available where we resided. Beijing, an international city, offered top quality care, but this was standard procedure for all employees and their families who lived outside of their home countries, and it had been nearly a year since we left our last address.

An eighteen-hour fast had induced a hunger headache, and the prospect of lunch dominated my thoughts as I anticipated a reward of sweet dumplings. Eager to finish the chore, I pulled off my shirt, lay flat on the table, and allowed Nurse Shai to place the sticky tabs on my chest, arms, and legs. She operated the machine, viewed the paper, tore it up, and began again. Three times the paper ripped. Excusing herself, she left the room.

Hmmm—trouble with the machine? I wondered.

Seconds later, three figures shuffled in. The one wearing an official white coat uncrumpled the papers, scrutinized the zigs and zags, and then carefully rearranged the line of her lips before facing me. "How do you feel, Shannon? Are you having any chest pain?"

Suddenly aware of disturbed expressions, my naked torso, and the eyes upon it, I shifted uneasily, covering my chest. "I feel fine—just a little embarrassed."

The doctor patted my shoulder gently. "I'm Dr. Grey. We want to run your ECG again for accuracy."

Two tries later, apprehensive glances confirmed Dr. Grey's concern. "I'm sorry, Shannon. We need to keep you here. I can't ethically allow you to leave the hospital with these results. Please follow Shai. She'll take you to a more comfortable room while we make arrangements."

Globally, we measure time by the solar year: twelve months or 365 days, beginning January 1. Many Eastern countries also acknowledge the lunar year, which is approximately the same length as the solar year and is based on the moon's cycle. Then there is the school year, a period for children to begin and end a stage of learning.

For me, that day marked a new calendar, measuring life-changing events in three consecutive May windows, the ECG being the first and writing this book the third.

However, first allow me to paint the backdrop before returning to Beijing, or how will you know what atmosphere I breathe?

Forty-three years ago, I emerged in the heart of the Bible belt into contradictory arms. My naked cries called to an atheist father and I suckled milk from a woman not quite ready to announce her homosexuality. Ill received by her evangelical neighbors, Mother exited the closet a few years later with a suitcase in hand. Bidding my brother and me adieu, she left in search of her identity.

Please don't weep, for odd beginnings are not necessarily depressing. In my case, it was rather the contrary. Unlike in traditional "evil stepmother" fairytales, I discovered that far more angels than demons reside in our world. One of them married my dad near my sixth birthday, offering me fifty percent more cuddles than most children I tagged on the playground.

Barely a year separated my brother, Austin's, grand entrance and mine. Due to our closeness in age and his passive nature, we cooperated as equals. If pressed, I admit I exploited this from time to time. Either way, he usually was at my beck and call.

I call my dad's second wife Mom, because that is what she is. Recognizing a need to expand our social network, Mom and Dad dipped their hands into Mother Nature's clay and molded two more playmates for my brother and me. Being much younger, they adapted eagerly to any role I chose for them. Big-sister esteem carried privileges. "Being in charge" was one of them.

As with many youngsters, in addition to my siblings, my imaginary friend stood loyally by my side. I called him God. We spoke our own language and he always reveled in my activity of choice. My mischievous nature never stumped him as I whispered questions and thoughts too bold to communicate to others. Perhaps the ease of this relationship, combined with a churchless childhood, instilled my lack of reverence later in life.

Once puberty arrived, I only approached my friend, God, occasionally when I required a favor. However, my aspirations to "fit in" led me to abandon such child's play.

Later, at seventeen, a friend invited me to her little country church. The preacher's wise words mixed with soothing melodies, and the camaraderie of my peers captivated my spirit. From that point on, I accepted the pew that waited.

Because diverse cultural rulebooks sat upon my childhood bookshelf, my adult years were graced with an expansive outlook. I honored this gift, but tucked it away from others' sight for years, unsure of how they would perceive it.

Over time, I permitted glimpses when I felt absolutely sure

the receiver would not react with fear. Friends with religious backgrounds different from my own merited more trust. Assuming that their acceptance of me did not rely on the same laws, I felt less confined. Their ears surely rang with my brash questions and the statements that were taboo in the sanctuaries of my childhood companion.

That said, as genuine friends do, God always forgave my audacity. He seemed to understand and accept the part of me that others did not. Despite his "fearsome" reputation, God is actually a pretty cool guy!

On the other hand, tradition raised my husband. Charles' chubby baby feet kicked the seat before him when his minister bellowed, "Let us be as children in the eyes of God!" His kindergarten fingers gripped crayons tightly as the Sunday school teacher instructed, "Please stay within the lines." He folded his hands while Mommy thanked their Father for their daily bread.

Yet one must be somewhat open-minded to marry a gypsy like me. Thus, when he requested my hand in marriage, he offered his in return, for compromise seals itself in a handshake. Our wedding photo shows bride and groom glowing cheek to cheek. However, over the years, this image merged, portraying one being blended from the features of two. Nonetheless, our natures required no compromise, for both already craved the taste of adventure.

Thus, with a decisive itinerary, Mr. and Mrs. Rigid-Irresolute jumped hand in hand onto a boat to "Elsewhere." Shortly after we embarked, the wind blew our plans into the churning sea. We have been winging it ever since, through years of travel and three kids.

We have also met the most interesting people along the way. Many granted us friendship, expanding our gratification and awareness of life's essence. After years of feeding from the wisdom of others, I often wondered why my invisible buddy placed that infamous tree in his garden to begin with. Certainly, He had his reasons. Was Eve not quite mature enough to accept the wisdom? Perhaps he was only waiting for her permanent teeth to grow in before offering a bite.

Just before our eighteenth "I do," and following a long stint in Africa, Charles and I packed our bags once more, along with the three other mouths we fed, and journeyed from Angola to the East China Sea, where life set my table with unforeseen circumstances. Each ingredient placed itself before me when the time was right to concoct what I am today.

Shortly after we disembarked, destiny sprinkled three sages into Asia's cuisine: Ling, Bonnie, and Adya. As each of them offered a unique flavor and nutrient, empty spots felt satiated as they appeared in my path.

Ling approached me first, introducing herself at an AGAS dinner party just after we arrived. As Vincent, her husband, worked and traveled with Charles, they also became close companions. As empty nesters, Ling and Vincent rented a sky-rise apartment downtown, enjoying Beijing's urban atmosphere and nightlife. Their appearance and energy camouflaged them in a younger scene. I often professed to Charles my wish to imitate their fun-loving attitude when our own kids left home.

I ran into Bonnie on the first day of school and requested directions to the bus stop. We met again later that day when we retrieved our children. While waiting, Bonnie and I fell to chattering, discovering only two weeks' difference in our arrival in Beijing. We lost track of time until small fingers tapped our backs—arms over shoulders, our giggling daughters. Apparently, they shared the same teacher and the two had devised a plan to introduce their moms on the ride home. It seemed that fate beat them to it.

Seven months elapsed before Adya came into my life. My oldest son, Michael, acquainted us through fever. Mono had infected his schoolmates and his girlfriend. Putting two and two together, I linked his lingering sore throat and fatigue to the virus and made an appointment. Upon our arrival, a young woman introduced herself as Dr. Adya and led us into her office. Throughout the exam, small talk revealed that she had moved from Ecuador to China around the same time that we arrived. When I inquired whether she had met many people, Adya confessed that work and two small children consumed most of her time. Thirty minutes also revealed an interesting and witty woman whom I wanted to know, so I invited her for coffee. She accepted and over time became the sister with whom I imagined growing up.

The evening after my hospital scare, fried egg noodles and spicy Sichuan tofu filled the house with aromas, making my mouth water. I followed my nose through the swinging door of our kitchen to find Ayi Ju, our maid, chopping vegetables. Her plump little body stood firmly by the counter as she minced peppers, onions, and carrots.

She kept her hair short and never wore make-up, most likely for convenience. A hard life painted many more years on her face than the forty-three she boasted. Nevertheless, her rosy cheeks and full lips presented a pleasant face and Ayi's wisdom and appearance harmonized. Compared to my three children at ten, thirteen, and fifteen, her son of twenty-five provided her with experience far beyond my own.

This lady took her title seriously, doting upon and fretting over each member of the Love household like a warm-hearted aunt. Ayi Ju brought a certain hospitality into our home that we would not have enjoyed otherwise, and on days like today, I especially appreciated her. "Ni meimiao" *You are so wonderful, Ayi.*

Continuing her chore, she beamed.

I leaned over her shoulder, sniffing the air and rubbing my belly. "*Hao*, Ayi!"

Her bright smile widened, exhibiting the teeth underneath, as she greeted me, "Xie xie. I glad you like."

Ayi's grin faded slightly as her glance became a gaze. "Okay, *Tai Tai*?"

I recognized the concern in her eyes, so I patted her gently in reassurance. "Wo hao" *I'm okay.*

I was so thankful for Ayi and our relationship. Almost all expats and middle class Chinese citizens enjoyed domestic help, but they did not always get along with one another. Ayi Ju seemed comfortable with us and I was grateful. Our relationship did not begin easily. It took time to cultivate. In the beginning, Ayi seemed aloof. She worked hard, but rarely smiled. I suspected past employment experiences had sketched some of the lines in her face. Elitist attitudes burrow their way into every culture, and our expat community was not immune. Ayi Ju, an intelligent woman, recognized the injustice. Although she wore cotton rather than silk, she wore it with pride, and her dignity shimmered in her eyes and sang through her voice. It was not store bought. I admired her, and she understood.

Charles, the kids, and I all gathered around the dinner table of our home. It felt good to be there—our little palace, as I sometimes referred to it. For, although the exterior resembled every other cookie cutter, three story villa in Beijing Riviera, boasting yellow stucco and a Spanish tile roof, we made this undistinguished box our own.

AGAS recognized the value that a personal touch added to one's quality of life and allowed a generous shipment for each of our overseas moves. We took advantage of this privilege, placing favorite pieces of furniture and art collected from our travels in each one, granting us the opportunity to create an abode with personality rather than acceding to the sparse furnishings our landlord provided.

Thus, we watched television on our cozy couches and placed our feet on the coffee table we selected ourselves.

Charles and I also splurged from time to time; one such incident was the table we ate on—a specially designed, dark walnut masterpiece built by a local Beijing artisan. The chiseler coupled traditional Chinese artistry with a modern western motif, rendering a style that would mingle well with the rest of our hybridized home. Thus, in accordance with our decor, we delved into our supper with chopsticks while slurping iced tea from Ikea glasses.

Don, my middle child, began the discussion. "Mom, why did you have to stay at the hospital? Dad said it was just a follow up on your physical. Is everything alright?"

I knew my kids were too smart and too curious to accept an answer as simple as that, and I was prepared to expound. "It was just a fluke with one of my tests. They wanted to investigate it a bit more, but couldn't find anything wrong."

Michael would not let it rest. "What type of tests?"

I stole a glance at Charles, who cleared his throat. "It was a little something with your Mom's ECG."

"What's an ECG?" Jean inquired.

"It's an electrocardiogram, a device the doctor uses to check the electrical activity of your heart," her father told her.

"Shocking!" Michael teased.

Jeans eyes popped. "Did they shock you, Mom?"

I shot Michael a stern look before addressing my daughter. "No, honey. It doesn't hurt, and everything turned out fine. Don't worry."

Don's face relaxed. "I'm glad you're okay, Mom."

My older child added sincerely, "Me too."

Charles reached across the table and squeezed my hand. "We're all relieved that everything turned out alright."

Genesis

Despite my lack of transparency with Christian friends, Bonnie became an exception, although our religious views differed vastly. Bonnie's biblical knowledge and dedication to the church far exceeded mine. These qualities, coupled with her community service, devotion to her family, and the hand she offered continuously to those around her embodied the spirit of a saint. She would surely eschew such a title, however, as I would add modesty to the list. As a soccer player in college, Bonnie turned down the opportunity to play professionally and opted for a more domestic route. After observing this impressive mother of four and adoring wife, I suspect she made the right choice. However, as we both favored exerting energy over conserving it, we preferred to chat while in motion. Morning walks triumphed as our top choice, and I can honestly say that "Hum Drum Avenue" was never our path. Why? Because Saint Bonnie had a wild side and she took it to the streets! Each time we stepped away from our neighborhood, Bonnie led us to some obscure area, far off the beaten path. I recall stray dogs, *hutongs*, country roads, and an absence of foreign faces like mine. As a geographically challenged person, I could neither return to them nor find them on a map. I can only concede that she eventually delivered me to my front door.

Bonnie also pumped runner's blood into our walks. Generally not a competitive person, I do pride myself on a few things. One of them is my pace. Until that point, I held bragging rights as the fastest walker around—well, at least around me. Past companions hailed the "sidewalk drill sergeant" they endeavored to accompany. However, I abdicated that honor humbly to Bonnie and those rocket-fueled feet of hers!

Our minds pumped even more iron than our bodies. Words wrangled around family, and religious and philosophical issues. My bohemian language mixed with Bonnie's ceremonial dialect to yield something I like to call acumen, so that when my tour guide finally led me back to the spot from which she had taken me, I savored the endorphins released by the mental, physical, and emotional training.

"Thanks for taking care of Jean last week." She'd kept my daughter the day I was detained at the hospital.

"Anytime. Andrea enjoyed hanging out with her."

"Yeah, but you also have three more to keep up with."

"The girls entertained themselves. And they're pretty good about including Valerie."

"I hope so. Since Jean's the baby at home, I worry how she treats the younger ones."

"She's no problem—really."

"Thanks, Bonnie."

My friend paused for a minute before broaching the subject. "Are you okay?"

"Yeah—just a little scared by my ECG."

"But all is good?"

"Yeah."

"Is there anything I can do?"

Smiling. "Not necessary. Except, maybe one thing."

"Name it."

"A new pair of legs. Mine can't keep up with yours!"

Divinity has suggested eternally assorted grains to nurture my mind and soul. From my earliest childhood, each individual who crossed my path has shown me a new avenue I had not previously considered. Therefore, when my path converged with Adya's, I was somewhat surprised to meet a strain of barley of which I was unaware, that of the Baha'i faith. Raised in Florida, not far from my old stomping ground, my friend followed the rules and path of Baha'u'llah with the same commitment that her neighbors did

Jesus. Adya's stories of her Savior and His ideals fascinated me, and by positioning her to the left of Bonnie, Beijing offered me two vantage points from which to peer at the same star.

That said, Adya appreciated my naughty nature and even played along from time to time. One such moment happened in a pottery shop. Perusing the various hand-painted plates, cups, and vases, we happened upon their bathroom. As gracious diplomats, the owners offered what we expats refer to as a "Chinglish" interpretation, a translation that doesn't quite hit the mark. To be fair, I am sure my Chinese friends have a nickname for our droll attempts to speak Mandarin.

Pointing to the sign above a curtain separating the toilet from the patrons, Adya nudged me. "Hey, Shannon. Do you need to use the 'private area'?"

The adolescent boy lurking too close to the front of my mind popped forward. "Not sure. You think they keep it covered?"

"I hope so. Wouldn't want to cause a scene."

"Think I'll wait—probably gets too hot in there." Thereby, our conversation would roll straight into the gutter, dubbed "Shannon's Humor."

Adya also slapped my wrist when she caught me sneaking more than my share from the cookie jar. If life offered multiple choices, she informed me when option 'A' was the correct answer. I didn't always heed her advice, but I often did, respecting that her judgment and intentions were good.

Only a select few folks care enough to risk ruffling our feathers and relationship to impose an uncomfortable, "I don't think you should," and then lend us their car after we have run the red light anyway. Adya ranked in that category and that is why I call her my sister.

When the bell rings "SUMMER!" at an international school, we expats throw on our Hawaiian shirts, Bermuda shorts, and sandals—or parkas, depending on which side of the equator our compass points. Meanwhile, *Home is Where the Heart Is* serenades us. We shout "Seeyalaters" as we depart, promising to bring back a slice of Momma's homemade pie to those stuck at the office. Then we forget this other world for a couple of months while drinking in refreshment from our homelands.

Charles requested that his slice be placed on ice. Summer duty would keep my husband in Beijing the first two weeks, though he was permitted to join us later, common practice for many expatriates. For me, part of this experience was longing for my missing partner. How could I not? This man had been in my life since fourth grade. I recall our first kiss just a year after we met at the age of eleven—truth or dare. Not to be deemed a coward, I made the audacious choice.

"Your lips must touch for ten seconds," our friend mandated on the playground steps. Holding our breath and squinting our eyes, Charles and I puckered. His full lips—so warm—held me. From that moment, I anticipated with passion the heat his mouth would dispense on mine.

My mind summons his first "I love you"—uttered during our senior year of high school. Twelve months before, Charles had suffered a football injury that resulted in a detached retina, leading to blindness and ultimately the expulsion of his right eye. Throughout his surgeries and recovery, I stood by his side loyally, unyielding, with daily phone calls and incessant visits. Thus, by offering my fidelity at Charles' most vulnerable moment, I finally unzipped the heart of my childhood crush.

Even now, twenty-one years later, I waited for him for fourteen days, dreaming of my fingers stroking his silken, russet wisps at night—laying my head on his broad shoulders. I visualized him enfolding me in his arms, telling me about his day in that voice that invariably seemed deeper when it was only the two of us. Yes, after all these years, this man still made my heart flutter.

Thus, on the day he arrived, I made an effort to award him with that same reaction. After shaving my legs and adding that extra special touch to my hair and make-up, I retrieved him from the airport in my sexiest sundress. In return, my rumpled, jetlagged man sprang to life when his sweetheart jumped into the arms he opened, planting a kiss just after his feet landed on Alabama soil. However, that was to be our only time alone, as countless relatives waited anxiously to set eyes upon the man they could see for just a brief spell each year.

As much as I would love to offer a steamy car scene, a certain condition slipped out of my husband's briefcase, choking the passion between us. I'm sure she wore a smirk while introducing herself. "Hello, Shannon. Nice to see you again. Do you remember me? I'm Health Concerns."

"What are you digging out of that bag of yours—a surprise for me?" I grinned.

Charles frowned. "Yeah—but not the kind you like." He waved the papers in his hand. "These are your medical orders. AGAS set you up with a cardiologist here."

"Why? I thought we settled it last month."

"They're not satisfied with the results."

"Why not? Everything looked great."

"Everything but your ECG."

"Lots of people have abnormal ECGs, Charles."

"Yes. But since yours was normal a year ago and seems to be evolving, they're concerned."

"Crap! When is it?"

"Tomorrow."

"You're kidding me."

"It's just a day or two—shouldn't take much time."

"Then you'd better find a way to relax me, mister!"

Chuckling, he acquiesced. "I can do that. But you may have to wait till midnight—or else Aunt Sue might follow us for another round of dominoes."

The next morning I threw on exercise attire, gulped down cereal, and extended puppy dog eyes to the coffee I could not drink. Then Charles and I headed to round two of my heart race: an obstacle course, engineered by a treadmill, syringe poking chair, black and white ultrasound, red and blue ultrasound, and a fancy coffin. Of course, I wore sticky tabs the entire time, with strings attached. As a disciplined exerciser, I smoked the run. That goop they stuck in my arm nearly put me out, though.

In the end, it was a day of, "Hmm…" Frown. Side glance. Test one. Test two. Test three.

"No chest pain?"

Test four. Test five.

Then a follow-up reply of, "Sometimes these things happen. All results contradict your ECG reports. We can't find anything wrong with your heart, Mrs. Love."

Charles and I left the hospital to enjoy our vacation and the rest of our lives.

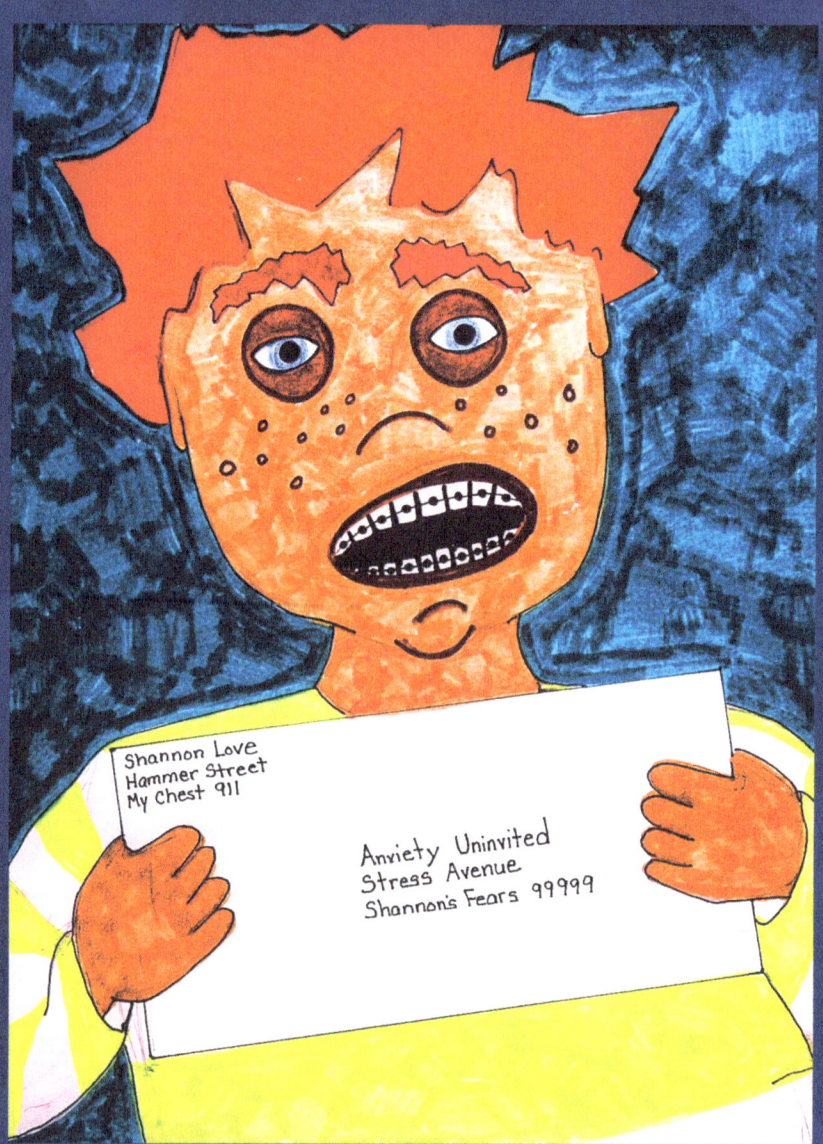

Chapter Two:

Fidgeting

ALTHOUGH THE CARDIOLOGIST'S office extinguished my attacks of palpitation, it did burp one little hiccup. Apparently, my blood analysis lacked thyroid hormones. Furnishing a pill replacement, they suggested I follow up after returning to Beijing. AGAS'medical team grabbed the ball and carried it across the ocean for me. It landed in the arms of Dr. Armaan Rostami, one of the top doctors at Beijing Global Care Hospital.

Before seeing the white coat, I first submitted my arm to Nurse Yi.

"One-twenty over seventy-five. Very good, Mrs. Love. Why are you here today?"

"My last set of tests implied hypothyroidism. The cardiologist recommended I follow up here."

"I'll let the doctor know you're here. Please have a seat."

As I waited outside Dr. Rostami's door, I couldn't help but notice the many *hats* draped across it. Which one would he wear today: pulmonologist, internal medicine, or critical care?

In my case, he grabbed all three.

With the finesse of a magician, he led me to the seat beside his desk. His business-like fashion and sparse eye contact commanded deference. I found myself intimidated by his presence, an unusual experience for me.

"I understand you're here for a thyroid check. How long have you been on medication?"

"A little over a month."

"Have you ever struggled with your weight?"

"No. I eat healthy and exercise regularly. I would say that overall, my metabolism has been fairly normal."

"Thyroid activity can fluctuate. It could've simply been a slow day. Let's take a blood sample and see what it looks like."

"I'm fine with that."

"On another note, I received an email from your husband's employer. They're concerned about your ECG results and would like me to perform a series of tests."

Not again!

"I've been through this with two other doctors. They both concluded that my heart's in good health."

"They're probably right. I'll try to make it as painless as possible. Can you tell me about your personal and family medical history?"

"Heart disease runs in our gene pool. My father suffered a heart attack in his fifties, my biological mother requires full time care after her stroke at sixty-two, my grandmother's first heart attack hit her at forty-nine, and my older brother died from one at thirty-six. Needless to say, this frightens me."

"Let's set up an appointment in two weeks. By then, we'll have your thyroid results and can proceed with the rest."

It soon became evident why he wore the third hat on top of those silver-speckled black waves. Years of experience informed him that the fragile spirit sometimes requires care of the most critical nature in matters of health. Our first meeting was the only time I saw his stoic side.

Dr. Armaan Rostami became much more than a medical

practitioner to me. Over a period of nine months, he grew into my physician, counselor, teacher, confidant, and friend. Long after my final appointment, his charitable and perceptive words assisted me through the most difficult chapter of my life.

Rubbing their sore behinds after an unexpected shot, children grab their mommy's loving hand for comfort and a trip to the ice cream parlor. That's how I knew someone had forewarned Charles of the punch Dr. Rostami had delivered, as he surprised me in the waiting area with a kiss and romantic dinner plans.

We boarded our van, requesting that Mr. Peng, our driver, take us to Forbidden Italy, a quaint little Italian restaurant operated by an authentic Sicilian in a secluded *hutong* north of the city center. He dropped us off on a corner of a walking street and we made our way down the twisting alleys, lined with antique traditional courtyard homes that, in recent years, were occupied by a mix of small shops, restaurants, and residences.

As the sun set, Charles and I strolled through the artery of this ancient address, just in time to watch old men gather around miniature outdoor tables in groups of four, drinking beer, and throwing down their tiles in a game of *Mahjong*, while old women paired up in their card game—*Dou Di Zhu*, they called it—keeping one eye on their treasured and only grandchild and the other on their hand.

After ten minutes of winding this way and that, we thought we might be lost, but just as we mustered up the courage to interrupt one of the locals and ask for directions, we saw the restaurant's name painted above large wooden doors. Italian ambiance and cuisine invariably set a romantic tone. This night was no exception. Still, after the waiter led us to a candlelit table by the window, I had to move the elephant before relishing our intimate moment.

"You knew."

Charles sighed. "Yes."

"Why didn't you tell me?"

"Because I knew how you'd react."

Controlling my demeanor, I responded. "I'm actually quite calm, in case you haven't noticed."

"I didn't want to worry you unnecessarily ahead of time."

Rolling my eyes, I said, "Thanks."

Charles grasped my hands across the table, folding his own over them. "AGAS is just being extra cautious. They assume a certain amount of responsibility when they take you away from your own country."

"I get that. This just seems a little excessive."

Sucking in his breath, Charles again breathed out. "It's your heart, Shannon."

"First you order me not to overreact. Then you declare it a serious matter. That's not fair, Charles."

"I'm just saying that certain health conditions receive priority over others. Please take it easy, darling."

My lungs tightened to the air they held until I finally relinquished. "Okay—and it won't take long?"

"It should be similar to the last two times."

Relaxing, I grinned, rubbing his leg beneath the table. "Then I suspect a rapid pulse won't cause too much damage."

"Slow down, baby," Charles teased. "Unless you want me to request the check before your main course arrives."

"Listen, gorgeous, *You* are my main course. But I need a little eggplant parmesan as an appetizer." After that, we relegated health concerns to the back burner, addressing matters more important, like my brown eyes and Charles' dazzling smile.

A few days later, I met my friend, Ling, for lunch at our favorite sushi restaurant, located in Sanlitun, Beijing's Yuppyville. It featured various upscale shops and cafes and catered to the young, posh crowd. We middle-aged expats crashed their party daily. It was

Fidgeting

a necessary evil to support the stores the younger folks could only afford as a hangout. As the mother of one of them, I tried to limit my social activity to the daylight hours, so as not to encroach upon his territory.

Just as Bonnie and Adya offered lookout towers to heaven, Ling was my air gauge. When too much hot gas built inside of me, she knew just how to release it with her laughter, energy, and jovial outlook. Ling's gift of placing life's celebrations under the Christmas tree year round never ceased to lighten my mood. I can honestly say that at no time have I seen or heard her say or act in a contemptuous manner—and she was so much fun!

So, chopsticks in hand, Ling and I pulled out the gloomy pieces, devouring more jubilant ones, as we gabbed effortlessly about whatever fell from the tips of our tongues. Today it was our craziest vacation experiences.

"Seriously?" I replied. "How old were the boys?"

"About five and seven," Ling responded.

"And they didn't notice?"

"Little kids don't pay attention to those sorts of things."

"You're telling me that you had no idea it was a nude beach."

"Not a clue. I'm not fluent in Spanish, and Barcelonian's speak Catalan anyway. We couldn't read the sign."

"So what did you do?"

"Well, I kept my bathing suit on."

"Did people look at you funny?"

"It was just a bunch of old people. I guess at that age, they could care less."

I laughed. "I suppose you're right. How long did you stay?"

"Until the boys tired of playing in the ocean." Ling threw me a playful grin.

"So, what about you?"

My return required no rumination. "It involves a gorilla and a chase."

"And you're alive to tell it?"

"Yep. It's quite funny, actually."

"I'm all ears."

"I joined three girlfriends in Rwanda on a gorilla trekking expedition back in 2010. Our tour guide briefed us on how to respond if we offended one of the silverbacks."

"Run for your life?"

I shook my head. "Actually, he informed us that they're not aggressive and to just slowly back away facing our perpetrator—but in the moment, that doesn't come so easily."

"I take it you were chased."

"Yeah. As I was filming one of the mamas who was breastfeeding her baby, the silverback must have felt I invaded their space. He ran toward me, beating his chest."

"What did you do?"

"Exactly the opposite of what I should. I screamed, 'Oh shit!' and ran, fell flat on my face in the mud, and dropped my camera."

"Did he attack?"

"Nah, he just cussed me out. Everyone else in the group got a good laugh though."

The following Saturday, Charles, the kids and I piled ourselves into the van for a morning of Chinese luxury—a massage. Specifically, we indulged our feet.

Intellectually, Charles' finance and engineering background placed his technically structured way of thinking far from mine. However, his sociable demeanor and respect for the arts made us very compatible. His right brain and my left never ran low on conversation, even after eighteen years of marriage.

That said, I tended to avoid unpleasant topics. Priding myself on being an optimist, I didn't like to complain, not even to my husband. This worked well for most of our marriage. However, it kept one component of our relationship shallow, while also leading to a certain degree of awkwardness when unfortunate issues arrived. Today would turn into one of those moments.

My husband juggled his employer's demands and our family's needs like a champion. Watching from the sidelines, this spectator marveled—"You make it look easy."

"What?" Charles wondered.

"You manage offices all over China and then come home to help Michael with his calculus."

"You take charge of our home life so well, it takes a big load off of me," he replied.

"But you're a very hands-on dad. And you work twelve-hour days."

Shaking his head, my lover corrected, "More like thirteen."

"And you travel a ton."

Charles conceded, "Yeah, I never really get used to that."

"How do you manage everything so smoothly?"

He paused, as if to consider his confession before blurting it out. "I'm a ball of stress."

Taken aback, I replied, "But you seem so put together."

"On the outside."

Considering his statement, I wondered if my other half was not so different from me. Could I broach the topic I generally avoided with him? "Do you struggle with anxiety?"

"Horribly! It's what keeps me up at night."

Admittedly, this likeness consoled me. "I have the same problem."

Astounded, Charles replied. "You're kidding me! I know you're a little excessive with your health, and…" He searched the back of his brain. "You do seem to toss in your sleep lately. Other than that, you're the most happy-go-lucky person I know."

"That's just it. These tests: they've gotten the best of me."

Charles sighed. "You'll be okay, Shannon. You need to stop obsessing over it."

I acknowledged this part of me my husband would never understand and feigned the response he wanted to hear. "Yeah, it'll all be over soon anyway."

He tapped his fingers, informing me of his desire to switch subjects. "Yes, it will."

So I did. "The kids sure are quiet over there—must be enjoying their massages."

Then there was Adya. She perplexed me with this new religion of hers, and we discussed it regularly. Today it commenced on her couch.

"It's not that young, Shannon," Adya explained.

"Less than two hundred years is pretty fresh by comparison to other faiths. Still, I can't believe I've never heard of it."

"You're from the Bible belt, a pretty homogeneous area."

"Yeah, but I've been away for nineteen years. I thought I'd seen most of them. And you're not even a first generation?"

"Nope. A fairly long line on my dad's side."

"Very cool. And Baha'is believe that all the major religions encompass the same God?"

"Yep."

I leaned back, scratching the thought I felt niggling in my head. "You know—that's kind of what I think."

Adya voiced a speculation she had held tightly until that moment. "Then you think like a Baha'i, Shannon."

"I'm not convinced. Religion's a bit slippery to me."

"What do you mean?"

"I can't seem to hold onto it."

"Why?"

"There's always some rule or idea that won't digest in my stomach."

Fidgeting

"So, are you Christian?"

"I am—sort of."

"What do you mean?"

"It's my outlet and background, as well as Charles'."

"But you aren't sure it's the one for you?" she inquired.

After pondering a response, I selected avoidance. "So, how's work going?"

The medical tests I thought would only take a couple of weeks had extended long past their welcome. I was beginning to lose my confidence in how things would turn out and a dormant condition from my past returned: anxiety. My chest initiated a few palpitations in its sleep and worked its way up to a constant dull ache. Consequently, I began to worry, which was causing the problem: but was it simple anxiety or heart problems?

Dr. Rostami displayed what looked to me like an electronic purse. "Do you understand how this works, Shannon?"

"Isn't it another ECG? I have to sleep with it?"

"Just one night. We need a full twenty-four hours of data. It'll help us correlate your ECG with all your daily activities, to better understand fluctuations and triggers."

Running my fingers through my hair, I stammered, "May I exercise? It's kind of my stress release."

My physician spoke with compassion. "I see this is causing you stress."

"I'm—I'm a little scared," I admitted, addressing the twisting hands in my lap.

"Have you considered talking to someone?" Dr. Rostami asked gently.

Refusing to meet his gaze, I replied, "I don't know. I'd feel silly."

"There's nothing silly about being frightened, Shannon. It's a legitimate emotion."

"I know."

Dr. Rostami wrote his prescription. "Here are two psychologists in this hospital. They're both excellent. Your mental health is as relevant as your physical."

Raising my head just enough to accept the sheet he offered, I whispered, "Thanks."

That evening, curled up in the chair beside Charles, I watched as he punched numbers on the computer keyboard. "Dr. Rostami suggested I see a psychologist."

Unfazed, Charles remained fixated on the digits he manipulated. "Damn! Our Solanta stock fell this week!"

"Charles, did you hear me?"

"Yeah. You want to see a shrink. Why would you waste time and money on that?"

"Money's not an issue. We have insurance."

"What in the world are you going to talk about for an hour?"

"I'm just a little nervous about all the tests."

At last, my husband turned away from his monetary investments to face his matrimonial one. "They're no big deal. Why are you blowing this out of proportion?"

"Charles, my brother *died* from a heart attack. Both of my biological parents have heart problems. This is very real to me!"

"You also exercise and eat like a rabbit. Trust me, you have *nothing* to worry about."

Balling my fists, I retorted. "I'm making an appointment."

My husband rolled his eyes. "Do what you want. You're going to anyway."

The following week, I entered one of GCH's smaller clinics. Searching for a spot where I could hide behind a book, I edged toward the far end of the waiting room couch, praying no acquaintances would show up. If anyone asked, my prepared response would be, "*Cough.* Just a little cold."

Fidgeting

Carefully arranging my novel and expression to project evidence of an intriguing story, I focused on a blur of words my mind refused to process. Just when perspiration began dribbling onto the pages in hand, a sandy-blonde man of medium build approached me with a pleasant smile.

"Shannon?"

"Dr. Baker?"

He offered his hand in an American shake, and then gestured behind him. "My office is this way. Will you follow me?"

Equating trepidation with weakness, I feigned the stride of a proud woman as he escorted me to his office. I accepted a seat, too lofty to notice the graciousness he undoubtedly projected. Then, as protection for the horse I sat high upon, when this stranger requested information I deemed *too personal,* I promptly fastened my lips.

After thirty minutes of crisp replies, Dr. Baker addressed the obvious. "Your main concern is anxiety, Shannon. Am I right?"

"Yes."

"And this is linked to the tests associated with your heart."

"That's correct."

Benevolently attending to the nose I was turning up, my psychologist suggested he guide me through a relaxation technique he called the body scan. As he agreed to participate, I played along, satisfied with his willingness to surrender his poise in exchange. Together we reclined our bodies and calmed our breath, focusing our attention on the starting point, our toes. Gradually, sweeping stress from our anatomies, we released it ultimately from the scalp's follicles.

Undoubtedly praying the weight he had lifted had lightened his recalcitrant patient's disposition, Dr. Baker waded into religious waters. "Shannon, have you considered using your faith?"

"What do you mean?"

Crossing his legs and arms as if to shield himself from possible attack, he expounded, "Do you follow a doctrine?"

Childhood memories of evangelical knocks upon our door, petitioning to save my father's soul from the depths of hell, encroached. This scene felt way too familiar, and I didn't like its direction. "That's no one's business."

"I simply meant that, if you have one, it could help."

Unwinding my unseemly contempt, I acknowledged his honest efforts. "Sorry—bad history with that. We attend church, I pray and talk to God regularly—I'm just not very religious."

"What do you mean?"

"I haven't found one I can wrap my arms around."

"If you could, it might ease your stress."

It was my turn to cross limbs. "I doubt that's possible or that you'll change my mind."

Studying the uncooperative client "requesting his services," my psychologist inquired, "Are you easily offended, Shannon?"

"Not at all!"

Scratching his chin, he pondered. "Then what provokes your reservations?"

"About religion?"

"About answering my questions."

"Repudiation."

"What do you mean?"

"The way I think doesn't seem to mesh with consensus. I'm more concerned about offending you." There. I'd exposed the vulnerability I disguised as aloofness and admitted to my fear of rejection.

At that moment, Dr. Baker grasped the key that would unlock my neglected disturbances. "Shannon, do you keep a diary?"

"I did as a child."

"It could offer you an outlet. A place to release—well—anything you want. It could be the ear you'll never offend."

His words inspired wonderment as they resonated with the urgency buried beneath my blind eyes, and by amazing grace, I

Fidgeting

could see! Offering sincere gratitude, I thanked him with, "Hmm—I might try that."

Journal
September 9

How does this work? Do I officially christen this as the first entry? Just in case, "I hereby appoint thee "Shannon's Journal!" Now what do I do? Tap the laptop three times? Perhaps I should say a few words.

Today my psychologist recommended I keep a diary. Since I enjoy the writing process more than sharing a bunch of crap with a man I barely know, I may have to fire him now that he has offered me a better alternative.

Oh-YES, I'm officially messed up enough for professional help. This heart thing cramps my style and torches my nerves. So here I am blabbing to you instead of a real ear. It's just easier.

Take a seat and I'll share a secret no one else knows. I'm afraid I'm going to die. Between my brother, Austin, my parents, and this health thing, my ticker's convinced it needs a new battery.

Now everyone seems to be offering me religion, which is another concern. It's as if they're afraid I'm going to miss the boat to heaven, dawdling over which one to take. I appreciate the offer, but I just plan to grab the Almighty's hand when the time comes. That being said, 'God, old buddy, can you wait a bit? I'm kind of comfortable down here.'

That's all for today. Maybe we'll chat again soon.

A few days later, Bonnie fetched me from the usual spot with the hot topic on her agenda. Honestly, religion intrigues me. It's just that my idea of it seems to rub against theological grains. That said, my gentle friend refused to bristle when she invited feedback.

Once my breath and step caught up to hers, I said, "Didn't you mention your parents' fiftieth wedding anniversary the other day?"

"Yep, it's next week."

"Bummer you can't be there. That's the hard part of being away."

She sighed. "Yeah, I wish I could," and then, brightening, she added, "but Omar, the kids and I did something for them."

"Really? What?"

"Remember the church my dad preaches at?"

"You told me about it."

"They're going to surprise them with a banquet next Sunday and one of the deacons contacted me and requested that we make a video."

"Were you okay with it? You hate being in the spotlight."

"This was different. No faces staring back—just the laptop."

"So how did it go?"

"It was actually very sentimental, something I tend to avoid with my dad. Being a preacher's daughter gets sticky, especially since I attended seminary school."

"That doesn't make it easier to relate?" I asked, surprised.

"Actually, kind of the opposite. We each have our own ideas, and they don't always mesh."

I laughed. "That's something I don't have to worry about."

Now it was her turn to query. "Your dad's an atheist. Don't you think differently?"

"Yeah, but he's pretty awesome about respecting our differences."

"He sounds like a terrific dad."

"He is. Growing up near more churches than shopping centers, people pitied me because of my 'heathen' father. What they didn't understand was that he displayed more kindness *and* less hatred than a lot of them."

Fidgeting

Bonnie chuckled. "I suppose the man on the edge always stands out."

"Yep, whether it's the reverend or the infidel!"

Exhilaration spins us into a brisk whirl, while tedium binds weight to our ankles. However, dismay blows ice through our open mouths, freezing us into position. I was officially disillusioned with these medical tests. I had reached my threshold and could take no more, wondering if AGAS' concern for my heart was becoming a self-fulfilling prophecy.

Dr. Rostami reiterated, "Shannon—did you hear me?"

"I'm confused. You just congratulated me on excellent test results. I've performed every stunt in the hamster cage. Now this?"

"Look at me, Shannon."

"I *am* looking."

"You've been staring *through* me for the last two minutes."

"When will this end?"

"They don't know you, Shannon. They see a name on paper with an evolving ECG red flag. To AGAS headquarters, you are a liability."

"How much more must we prove before I'm not?"

"I hope Hao Baojian hospital will help with that."

"Why do I need to go there?"

"We don't have the equipment necessary for a cardiac MRI."

"And then—no more?"

"I think."

"You promise?"

"You know I'm on your side."

Two days later, Adya and I met at a dinky little nail spa tucked in the back of a remote market in Lido, Beijing's mixing bowl for expats and locals. Pedicures, manicures, and massages cost fewer *yuan* and offered more indulgence than lunch. We often opted for this over our favorite restaurant.

Stretching our bare feet across the ottomans, we selected our colors and inhaled in preparation to gratify vanity and rapport. Because it was her day off, I dedicated every Tuesday to Adya. Whether we chose to pamper ourselves or just hang out at her house, I always looked forward to the time we spent together.

Yawning, she confessed that Caspar had kept her up most of the night. Adya and her husband, Roberto, had been weaning their little man from his crib over the past week, opening opportunities for night hunts through the house, Mommy and Daddy being his prey and their bed his hunting ground.

Relishing maternal opportunities that her profession withheld, my friend was always accompanied by her toddling sidekick. Today he exercised the spare energy he had sucked from his weary victim. Still, Caspar's chubby cheeks and adorable nature intrigued everyone around him, including the women who worked in the salon and me. Recognizing Adya's exhaustion, one of them scooped him up, sweeping him into distraction so Mommy could enjoy a few minutes of rest. She led him to a shelf standing in the corner. Unwilling to remove a protective eye from her son, Adya noticed a book he was tugging. Excited Chinese words pinged and ponged back and forth from her mouth and the young woman's. Although it was Asian to me, I could see Adya's enthusiasm as her drained body reawakened.

At the end of the discussion, she explained. "That's a Baha'i book. I asked her where she got it. She said it was hers. Apparently she's like me."

"Very cool! You've never seen her at your services?"

"She's Chinese. We're not allowed to meet in the same place."

"Oh, yeah, I forgot. That applies to our church, too." Then I

Fidgeting

asked, "Does that make it more comfortable to leave Casper with her?"

Muttering under her breath, Adya confessed, "I really don't like leaving him with anyone, unless I know them *very* well."

"If you and Roberto want to slip away sometime, I don't mind watching him."

"Thanks. I'll take you up on it." My friend mused in silence before changing the subject. "Shannon, if I ask you something, will you answer honestly?"

"Of course! Shoot."

"You know I work with Armaan," she eased in.

Crap! "Yes, and I already told you I was seeing him."

"I know, and he hasn't said anything to me. But I understand his specialty—and…" She burst out. "Well, you never talk about it. Why is that?"

This was the moment the room chose to spin, as it sometimes did when anxiety deemed my heart a trampoline, flipping into double somersaults from chest to head, until neither could take anymore. Making every effort to focus, I confessed, "Because it's humiliating."

Rotating her direction and attention one hundred percent to me, Adya exuded the confidence from which I shied away. "You're my closest friend here, Shannon. I tell you everything because I trust you. It's not fair to either of us, if it's just one way." She closed her eyes before she added, "Do you understand where I'm coming from?"

"You're right—sorry. It's just not easy for me. I tell you more than anyone else."

"Then talk to me. I'm not going to judge you, Shannon."

Why not? "It's all these tests for my heart. AGAS won't stop. And now I have this anxiety disorder—feels like I'm having a heart attack twenty-four hours a day. I'm so dizzy right now that it's hard to even carry on a conversation."

"Do you want me to go with you to your next appointment? You know, I *am* a doctor. I could be an extra set of ears."

Pride slapped another brick onto my wall of insecurities. The thought of my friend witnessing my tucked tail as I hung my wretched fear across Dr. Rostami's examining table assaulted me. "No worries." I managed a feigned ease. "He usually schedules while you're working."

Inspecting my closed door, Adya offered a window. "If you change your mind, I'm here."

Journal
October 11

Happy Birthday to me! Well, almost anyway. With a busy few days ahead, I suspect this is my last entry before the big four-two. Not so old in the scheme of things—nothing creams and hair color can't disguise :-) Ling's taking me to lunch Thursday, and Charles alluded to a surprise Friday evening.

I think he's planning something romantic. We need it. Things have been a little "off" lately. Work's stretching his nerves and this whole, "think I'm dying" thing frazzles mine. Could just be our midlife crisis. ANYHOW, it's nothing a triple X evening can't seduce back into the gutter of love!

But, argghhhh—first I have to go through that damn cardiac MRI. They scheduled it on my birthday!!! Can you believe it? Oh well, let's get it over with and celebrate with hubby afterwards.

Fidgeting

Approaching Charles' office door, dispirited, I skipped the general "How's it goings" I ordinarily directed to everyone I passed in an effort to prevent my nerve from slipping away. Somehow and somewhere between our house and AGAS, the diamond from my engagement ring had come loose and fallen out. Combing our van and retracing my steps confirmed that his matrimonial symbolic pledge was forever lost. To make matters worse, lately our relationship was sagging under the weight on our shoulders. In Charles' defense, he had attempted a facelift two weeks before, as he had arranged to take me to my favorite restaurant and a show on my birthday. Unfortunately, the contrast dye from my MRI earlier that day made me so sick that anything other than a twelve-hour nap was out of the question.

"Hey, you, ready for a night out?" He smiled, looking up from his desk.

"Hi."

"Uh oh. You look mad. What did I do?"

"Nothing. But you may want to skip dinner."

"What happened?"

Sticking my left hand under his nose, I said, "This."

Charles glared first at my ring, then at me. "How did you do this?"

Affronted, I retorted, "I didn't *do anything*!"

Composing himself and his voice, he restated, "How did this happen?"

"I don't know. I arrived a little early and decided to walk around downstairs before coming up. I just happened to look down and notice. Trust me, I looked everywhere—even went back to the van to search."

Closing his eyes and breathing in, my husband chose the high road. "Okay. Looks like there's nothing we can do about it. Let's go eat."

"You still want to?"

"Not really. But you're here—might as well."

We managed to share a cordial meal at a nearby Korean restaurant. However, disappointment deflated our moods and the conversation. We held hands to and from the car, reassuring ourselves that it was merely a material object, with no correlation to our love.

Finally, the moment had approached to close this chapter. I felt a huge weight lifted as I entered my physician's office to celebrate. Yes, it had been a rocky road, but I could now put these health concerns behind me.

Metallic blue wrapped the Godiva chocolate in the palm of his hand. Dr. Rostami beamed. "I officially present your Hearty Patient award."

"Why, thank you, Sir Armaan. I accept with humble gratitude." Chuckling, I tipped my pinky up, as if receiving a refined delicacy.

Humor lightened our consultations routinely. We each welcomed a little silliness to sweep that imperious somber tone into the corner from time to time.

"So, I'll see you in April."

"Just as a precaution?"

"Just as a precaution. We'll do an ECG and that's all."

"See you in April."

Elated, I hopped into the car, already dialing my phone.

"Hello. This is Charles."

"Hi, babe."

"You sound happy."

"Yep. All's good and finished on the heart issue. I'm ready to celebrate."

"What did you have in mind?"

"I thought we could see if Ling and Vincent would like to go out Friday night—maybe go dancing afterwards."

Fidgeting

"Dinner sounds good—dancing not so much."

"Come on, baby. I can ask Ayi Ju to stay the night. *Please*, I promise to reward you amply." Inserting carnal bribery.

Nothing.

"Charles—you there?"

"Yeah, I was just thinking."

Grinning, I teased, "Not too much, I hope."

"Why don't I come with you for dinner, then go home and watch the kids while you join Ling and Vincent. They could take you to one of the nightclubs."

"Aww, baby—I want you to go too. *Please.*"

"You know it's not my thing. I'd cramp your style. This way, Ayi Ju won't have to spend the night."

Hearing through the phone that his mind was made up, I capitulated. "Okay. Thanks for letting me go."

Chuckling, Charles chaffed. "Not sure if there's any 'letting' to it. Once you've made a decision, there's not much I can do."

Giggling, I assented. "Don't you forget it! Love you."

"Love you, too."

Three days later, Charles, Ling, Vincent, and I gabbed and laughed over French cuisine and red wine. I limited myself to one glass, reserving a spot for the second at the dance club; for me, more than that would yield dangerous effects.

Apparently, on that evening months of suppression required no booze for discharge. My two vivacious friends, unaware of what they were getting into, released this lioness onto the floor. Inebriated with rhythm and energy, I whirled under the strobe light, unconscious of time. Finally, at 3:00 a.m., they managed to drag me to their den, where Ling offered a spare bed, but bliss ravished my body and hoisted my eyelids upwards, as I replayed the pulsating beats and beams that had enchanted me. Abandoning sleep, I could have watched the rising sun, had my head not been stuck in the night before.

Chapter Three:
Offering

A TIME APPROACHES in each of our lives when Mortality chastises us, demanding what we have to show for ourselves. When she placed me on the bench, I offered my resume in my defense:

Shannon's Resume
1993-2013
Teacher
Mother

"And what are you doing now?" she demanded.
"I take care of my family."
Glancing at her notes, Mortality said, "I see here that from eight a.m. to three forty-five each day, your children attend school and that you have a full-time maid. Is this true?"
"Yes, but that's when I exercise."
"Mmm hmm. So you're saying that you work out almost eight hours a day?"
"Of course not! But I also run errands."
"Like what?"

"Like going to the grocery store."

"And how often do you do that, Mrs. Love?"

"Once a week."

Mortality pressed her body and message toward me, demonstrating the weight of its meaning. "Shannon, most likely, you're halfway to the finish line of life. You have a choice. You can either stop here, enjoying an early retirement, or you can continue. I think you have more to offer. What do you think?"

And then it hit me. A fulfilling existence is one that contributes in a positive way. I was not yet full. What could I add to my resume? Where would my skills and interests lead? I made a list.

Talents and Passions:

Education
Children
Relationships
Psychology
Philosophy
History
Reading
Writing
The Arts

After some thought, I narrowed it down to two options. Would I be Ms. Love, the history teacher or Shannon, the school guidance counselor? Counselor won, as my nurturing skills outweighed classroom management. Working with confiding teenagers seemed more natural than attempting to control a group of kids who might or might not be interested in what I had to say.

The following evening, while snuggling on the couch, I proposed the idea to Charles.

Leaning back in contemplation, my husband cross-examined.

"Wouldn't you rather return to teaching? You're so good at it."

"I want to try something different. Honestly, I'm not sure I have the energy for that anymore."

"So, what's your plan?"

"I thought perhaps an online program."

"You'll have to take the GRE. Most graduate programs require it now."

Confidence exited my gut, making room for uneasiness. "That's the intimidating bit."

Uncrossing his legs to pull me closer, Charles nuzzled his cheek against mine. "You can do it. You just need to study."

And so I did. The next six weeks involved researching, selecting, and applying for a graduate program—teaching myself and expanding forgotten skills, and extending my vocabulary. In late February, I had a classroom on my laptop, with two professors and schoolmates I would learn from and with, but never meet. Educational Psychology and Statistics wrote their names on the board, and thus began the construction of my kaleidoscope.

Swinging from my Ed Psych branch to Stats, I quickly appreciated the one on which I had a firmer grasp. Pedagogy, cognitive function, and behavior patterns intrigued me, while numbers and graphs produced more bafflement than understanding. I developed a certain respect and admiration for my husband's finesse in such matters.

Journal
February 28

It's been an exciting week. Adya and Roberto invited me to celebrate Ayyam-i-Ha (Baha'i's big holiday) with them on Monday. I took gifts for Avan and Caspar. They made a delicious meal and invited a few other Baha'i friends. I fit right in :-) We all talked about meeting up again soon. I'll try to sneak in between classes and studying. Oh yeah, I'm officially a school girl now! Yep. I began my courses this week and feel renewed! ANYHOW—I'll cross my fingers that my busy schedule will allow me to join the group.

Endorphins pumped their intoxicating potion through my brain as it exercised flabby areas into a lean, mean, thinking machine—well, at least a bit more than it had been. The exhilaration of new learning activated a long-lost spark within me. I felt twenty years younger! However, it came at a cost I did not yet realize.

My anxiety retreated a bit, but rather than leaving entirely, it transformed into a larger creature—mania. Nerve cells within my skull began to pump out extra doses of dopamine. In perfect proportions, this hormone makes us feel happy and motivated. However, escalated quantities act more like cocaine—throwing the uninformed victim into a high. You could say that Mother Nature became my drug dealer and I her user.

Early on, I had a blast! My mind seemed to absorb whatever it wished at a pace faster than light. Zest flowed through my veins, stimulating them with a young boy's vitality. However, this impulsive and hyperactive nature also influenced my judgment and ability to sleep, so that over time, long evenings at my computer replaced nocturnal dreams. A battery can only last so long without charging. Refusing to recognize this, I ran mine quite low.

Journal
March 21

Apologies for not writing much lately. Well, actually I have—just not in my journal. My Ed Psych class requires a lot of effort. I've kind of become obsessed with it. I find myself going overboard with the research questions in my assignments. This class

Offering

> *invigorates me. Charles is frustrated. He's mentioned several times that I need to stop putting so much into it and get some sleep, but I can't seem to pull myself away from the computer. I fall into a writing groove, and in the blink of an eye, it's two a.m. I should probably balance school more with family. Oh well, this is only temporary. In two years, I'll graduate and life will return to normal. Hopefully, they can be patient until then.*

Mania's shot of stamina lengthened my days, offering windows into various outlets. In addition to my graduate courses, Charles and I also attended an evening Bible study class. Every Wednesday night we met with other couples to eat, watch a theological video, and then break into small discussion groups. I found myself in a state of euphoria throughout each session and thought it was because I was touched by the message of the evening, and the compelling thoughts and stories flowing from the tongues of my peers.

Meanwhile, Adya shared more about the Baha'i faith. Its theme of all humanity being one family connected with my own values. I grilled her with questions, sometimes enthralled and at other times ready to debate. She answered each in earnest and without animosity. Deep immersion into both doctrines mixed with a large dose of unseen mania led me to fall inadvertently into a state of hyper-religiosity.

To intensify matters, I began to disconnect with Charles; our affectionate moments were reduced to meager, two sentence conversations. My husband always caught me "in the middle of something." He begged and waited for my attention, but could not compete with the high my mania provided. I made up for this lack of emotional intimacy by offering sensual favors, and justified the time away from my partner as a temporary sacrifice for the sake of our future. My priorities were converted to mayhem and for the first time in our marriage, Charles and I developed issues.

Around that time, our church presented a string of sermons that coincidentally bore remarkable resemblances to problems we struggled with at home. Early on, I dismissed it as mere coincidence. Then I became paranoid, speculating that people from our congregation might be talking about us behind our backs.

Days turned into weeks, and it seemed that the lower my tank got, the faster I wanted to accelerate. I must have whirled those around me into an exhausted state of observation. In brief moments of moderation, I considered how my pace and extra activities might affect my children; but then, once again, I became consumed by the exhilaration of mania and justified my frenzy with one excuse after another.

Fortunately, Adya's mom, Lois, paid a visit and brought me back down to Earth, at least temporarily. Because Adya worked, I volunteered to show Lois around Beijing. We hit some of the highlights of the city, such as Tiananmen Square, the Great Wall, the Temple of Heaven, and the Summer Palace. Hanging out with Lois was as much fun as a day with any girlfriend my age. Her bubbly personality, sense of humor, and easygoing demeanor created an easy chemistry between the two of us. As a matter of fact, I soon came to realize why Adya and I enjoyed one another so much. She reminded me a bit of my mom and I think Adya must have seen a similar likeness between Lois and me.

One day, after walking around for hours in the Temple of Heaven Park, climbing the stone stairs to peer into the circular structures, and testing out the altar's echo stones, Lois presented me with a gift—one that would not only acquire sentimental value,

Offering

but also soon help me through the struggle of my life. It continues to hold an honored place in my home and heart today. This very special tribute was a Baha'i prayer book, and I can honestly say that I could not have received it at a better time.

Chapter Four:

Obstacles

***WHY TODAY? I** should have come last week. This muddles everything!*

One grisly weekend botched my well-organized plan. I was to curl up early with a light read the evening before, roll out of bed to send the kids to school, and occupy the morning with solitaire and country music. Today was going to be my success story. I envisioned the nurse and me cracking jokes as I reclined my worry-free body.

"Astonishing!" she would exclaim. "How did you do it?"

"Do what?"

"Your ECG is perfect. It's—it's a miracle!"

"Diet and exercise. Where there's a will, there's a way."

Applauding me in clear wonderment, this young woman would then proclaim, "I can't wait to tell Dr. Rostami."

Who knows? One week earlier, this might have been the case, but then I would have no novel to narrate.

However, that's not what happened.

Instead, bad news positioned two coarse stones steadily within its sling. It then commenced to stretch, aim, and shoot, smacking this bird from her perch and hurling her flat to the ground.

A call from my aunt struck first. My biological mother had shifted into the fourth stage of renal failure. She didn't wish to trouble me, but after my brother's death, I was our mom's only living child and closest relative. An urgent flight home was paramount. My parents carried the second stone. My baby brother, Jason, had barely survived a car accident. He was in the intensive care unit and just out of emergency surgery for extensive damage to his internal organs and a severe head injury. They just weren't sure what his chances of recovery were.

As a result, two days later, when Dr. Rostami's nurse stuck tabs on my chest, my recalcitrant heart made such a ruckus, I simply could not control it.

Journal
April 15

What am I going to do? All these years I've kept an arm's length from Mother Jones. It was less painful that way. Now she's on her deathbed—or so I'm told. Austin, can you hear me? Why aren't you here now? You were always better with her. Guess you handed that torch to me. Thanks, bro! "Woman up and take care of her, Shannon!" Is that what you're telling me? How the hell do I arrange a funeral? More importantly, I need to get there in time to make things right between us. That's what I'll do, throw out all that emotional baggage. Things will be peaceful between us. I'm determined! Ramble, ramble. Today's about rambling. I'm a ball of stress and I need to spit it all out on these pages. Whether it makes sense or not is unimportant—just need a release. Pity party number two: Jason is hanging on to his life by a thread right now. Even if he survives, the doctors aren't sure how much brain damage he's suffered. He may never be quite

Obstacles

himself again. I'll be angry with you, God, if you allow anything to happen to my baby brother. It's not fair to strike the same family twice. If nothing else, think about his children. Don't do this to those poor girls!

The next day I tucked away my foolish pride and called Beijing Global Care Hospital, admitting what my body had been trying to tell me for some time. I was a mess! Too debilitated to help myself, I needed a professional. I requested Dr. Baker, but he was booked up for the next month. Instead, the receptionist recommended the department's head psychologist, Dr. Janet Hoi, who also served as a student advisor, and could only take appointments if I agreed to work with one of her students as well. She assured me that Dr. Hoi was top-notch and that I would receive excellent care. I accepted the earliest appointment available.

Three days after my ECG, Dr. Rostami surveyed my stiff upper lip and balled fists.

"Are you okay? You look tense."

"It's been a demanding week. May I ask your advice?"

"Of course!"

Blowing a sigh of relief, I disclosed my mom's and brother's health crises, picking his brain about when and how I should respond. He pointed out the variables attached to each of their ages and conditions, and proposed I weigh his professional advice with my own circumstances. His counsel presented the objective view of an expert, requisite to taking leave of one family, crossing an ocean, and caring for another.

Then he shed his other roles and focused on the one medical school bestowed. "We now need to discuss *your* health."

Placing two linear presentations in his lap, my physician gently but firmly charged,

"Look at these, Shannon."

Mountains, hills, and valleys expanded across the page, one row after another. Acquainted with their relevance to the battery powering my body, I scrutinized. It was no use. I could not decode this language.

"They are two minutes apart," he said.

Perhaps squinting would help.

"Look at this one—now the other."

Perplexity creased my face.

"Do you have chest pain?"

My knuckles whitened. "I have an anxiety disorder. The symptoms are identical."

"Should I contact AGAS?"

"No! Please don't! I can't—I can't do this again."

"Do you have anyone to watch the children if you need to go away for awhile?"

"I have an anxiety disorder!"

My brick wall refused passage. This conversation would go no further.

"Will you get help for your anxiety?"

"I made an appointment with Dr. Hoi."

He smiled. "I know her. She is very nice."

"I haven't met her yet."

"Make me a promise."

"What?"

"Allow us to couple your mental health with your physical—so we can get to the bottom of this."

"Okay."

But I never did.

Obstacles

"Thanks, Mr. Peng. I should finish in one hour." I stepped out of the car, passed through the revolving door of one of Beijing's deluxe hotels, and made my way to the winding stairs. According to the receptionist on the phone, BGC had tucked a mental health clinic in the basement. At the bottom of the stairs, two glass doors designated that this was the place.

After checking at the front desk, I found a spot to sit and observe the ultra-modern motif. Contemporary abstract paintings adorned the walls, coordinating well with sleek sculptures placed meticulously throughout the office. Even the teardrop-shaped chair I sat on was covered in Beijing's latest, chichi fabric.

Moments later, a very petite woman about ten years my senior approached the desk clerk for my whereabouts, then turned around and faced me. Her tender dark brown eyes spoke first, sending a dove-like gaze in my direction—then her voice. Warm velvety words floated from her mouth. "Hello, Shannon. I'm Dr. Hoi. Will you follow me to my office? Your other therapist, Jasmine, is waiting."

I trailed her into a dimly lit room with two fluffy wingback chairs facing a couch. The room's traditional look felt like my grandmother's living room—quite a contrast from the waiting area. Still, its inviting ambience offered a cozy and welcoming feel. Jasmine, Dr. Hoi's student, sat in one chair while her teacher took a seat in the other. I made myself comfortable on the couch, ready to face both women.

Was it me, or were Jasmine's hands shaking? She looked nervous.

Dr. Hoi smiled. "Jasmine here will be your primary psychologist. I'm more of an observer, but you'll hear me pose questions and make comments from time to time. In addition, as my secretary mentioned on the phone, we'll be taping your sessions. Are you satisfied with this arrangement?"

I nodded.

This time, desperation replaced the embarrassment I had disguised six months earlier. I was prepared to open up and talk.

Little did I realize the volume of withheld vomit I would pour out into that little room. Dr. Hoi and Jasmine endured the stench like champions with their gracious, composed responses.

Jasmine spoke. "Hi, Shannon. Thank you for trusting me. I'll do my best to uphold your confidence."

She's pretty. Such beautiful green eyes. Hmm, where is she from? I can't place her accent—the Netherlands maybe. "Thanks, Jasmine. Thanks, Dr. Hoi. I guess you know why I'm here."

Jasmine glanced over her papers. "I only know that you are here for an official evaluation. You think that you may have an anxiety disorder. Is that correct?"

She's from Denmark. That's definitely a Danish accent. I nodded.

"Can you tell us a little more about your symptoms, when they started, and what triggered them?"

Nope, I was wrong. That sounded Finnish. Oh hell—I'll figure it out sooner or later. "Sure, it all started last May." I recounted my symptoms and events until this point.

After that, she asked questions going back almost to birth, I suppose for insight about other factors that might be contributing to my problems; that part was a little uncomfortable, but not as much so as with Dr. Baker.

In the end, they determined that indeed I did suffer from an anxiety disorder. However, because they had no baseline by which to gauge me, my manic and paranoid states remained hidden. Dr. Hoi recommended that I see Jasmine on a weekly basis. I explained that I would soon need to leave town for a week to check on my brother and care for my biological mom, but that otherwise, I could clear my calendar.

Journal
April 20

I met Jasmine, my new psychologist, today. She's

actually a student under the supervision of Dr. Hoi. Very sweet and approachable. That made it easier. Since we were both a little anxious, neither of us felt intimidated by the other. We kind of got through the first session together. I can't believe how much I disclosed! We started with my childhood. Letting all that constipated crap out didn't hurt so badly after all. I feel a bit relieved.

That Friday, I joined a book club group. Mania had called "Why not?" and it was about my favorite novel, *The Source,* by James Michener. Already juggling more balls than I could handle, I might as well throw in another.

I usually relished book club as my favorite group activity, but this time was different. Friends and acquaintances appeared to be acting peculiar and making strange remarks. I felt as if I was the target of some sort of gossip, but wasn't quite sure what it was about.

That's when suspicion got the best of me. *What has everyone whispering?* I pondered obsessively. Then it became my extracurricular activity to investigate the origins of the slander of which I seemed to be the object. I ruminated about one scenario after another—even researching ideas on the internet.

All of this took a toll on my relationships. For the first time, this unassuming girl suspected ill will of those she held dear.

Ready for an evening walk, Bonnie met me on her front porch. "Hey. How's it going?"

"Good—busy. You?"

"You know—kids, church, social commitments with Omar's work. I'm hoping to stay close to home the next few weeks."

"You've kept yourself hidden lately."

We stepped into pace. "You're one to talk, missy. I never see you anymore. Where've you been?"

"School, kids, etcetera, etcetera."

"Omar and I are thinking about going to Thailand once school's out. Do you want to join us?"

Eager to appease, but not to add another trip to our overloaded summer, I passed the buck. "I'll talk it over with Charles."

As we turned the corner, Bonnie threw an unintentional hurdle in my path. "Hey, my friend, Obi, said you were in her book club group."

Indignation stiffened my muscles and clenched my jaws. "I doubt I'll go back to book club."

Surprised at my reaction, Bonnie responded, "Why? I thought you loved it."

"I do. But apparently there's been a misunderstanding."

"What happened?"

"That's the problem. I don't know! Everyone's acting funny around me, but no one wants to say why."

Bonnie leaned over to offer a hug. I accepted, needing a friend. Then we moved on to our ritual of catching each other up on the latest news of our kids.

Journal
April 22

So sorry, but I have to take a hiatus—too much going on right now between school, Bible study, psychotherapy, kids, and Charles. Plus, I need to work out how to get to Oklahoma to care for my mom. No time for journaling or sleep at the moment—catch up with both of you this summer.

XOX for now.

Obstacles

Barely managing to stay above water, I recalled my last appointment with Dr. Rostami. Those zigzags he had placed in my lap frightened me. Too alarmed to face the truth, I never made another appointment. I thought I might die, but fear prevented me from doing anything about it. Placing this concern on the back burner, I faced the ones I could do something about: school and my family.

Just before catching the jet that would stream me home, a special note delivered itself to my desktop: good news from Cindy, Austin's wife. We had last embraced seven years ago, just after his funeral. Now she wanted to come for a visit. Needless to say, I was delighted.

On the same day, my aunt delivered her own message. I felt the weight she bore from across the ocean.

Shannon,

Yesterday was one of the most difficult days of my life. I had to tell your mom what we're doing about her arrangements. Shawn from Valleyhill Funeral Home had to have her signature on the contract, because you and I don't have power of attorney. I prayed about it before I went in her room before Shawn got there. She did well at first, but later we both broke down. She said she didn't expect it to end like this. I stayed awhile and we held each other. Later I told her that I'd be with her to the end. I was so upset when I left, I couldn't think.

I look forward to seeing you in a couple of days.

Love you,
Aunt Peggy

Twisting My Kaleidoscope

Kissing Charles and the kids goodbye and promising to return with treats, I held tight to reunion's wings. Seven days in the States would bring peace with one mother, while strengthening the bonds with the other and the man she married, my father.

"Hey, you." My dad wrapped me in a bear hug at the Birmingham Airport. He looked tired. "How was your trip?" Then, scrutinizing my body, which was easily ten pounds lighter than last July, he added, "You look thin."

Returning his embrace, I ignored his comment and moved straight into my own investigation. "No problems on the flight. You look exhausted. How's Jason? When can you take me to see him?"

"If you're up for it, I'll take you there now. He's still in ICU, but they managed to stop the internal bleeding during surgery and the swelling in his brain has gone down. The doctors seem hopeful that he'll recover completely."

"Yes, I'd like to go. Thanks. When will they move him to a regular room?"

"As soon as they're sure he's stable—maybe tomorrow or the next day."

"I guess that's the extent of his prognosis?"

My father shook his head. "Shannon, trust me when I say that things are much better than a week ago. We didn't know what the outcome would be for awhile. Now, although it may not be easy or quick, at least we're pretty sure he's going to be okay in the end."

I studied my father's face. He had aged fifteen years in the past seven. At only sixty-four, Dad was much younger than the parents of most of my peers, but his once black hair had collected too much grey overnight, and those sea blue eyes had misplaced the enterprising vitality they once carried. Losing one son, and now almost another, had taken their toll on him. My dad had never forfeited his protective instincts over us. Although we were adults, he still felt responsible for our well-being—a heavy burden for anyone to carry. My heart ached for him. It ached for our whole family.

I leaned over and kissed my father's cheek. "Thanks for picking me up, Dad."

When we arrived at the hospital, I was greeted with hugs from my mom, both of my sisters-in-law and my brother, Glen. My mom and Jason's wife, Ellen, looked as if they had slept at the hospital. Glen and Marian, new parents of a fourth child, appeared surprisingly put-together, but they had always been the most organized of all of us.

I made my way to Jason's bedside. He looked better than I expected. Although he wore a nasty bruise on his face and had an I.V. drip in his arm, my baby brother greeted me with alert eyes.

I squeezed his fingers gently. "You gave us a scare, bro."

He managed a half smile. "Yep. I'd like to say I frightened myself too, but don't remember a thing."

"How do you feel?"

"They're keeping me pretty drugged up. It still hurts to move."

"I heard that they're moving you to a regular room soon. Are you ready for that?"

"Yep, I'm hungry—no hamburgers served here."

An hour later, my mom and I slipped away for some dinner and a little alone time.

"You look really thin," she pointed out. "Are you okay?"

Hmm. I wondered. *Why do my parents keep asking me if I'm okay? Did Dr. Rostami call?* I began to suspect that, in light of my last appointment with him, my physician had found a way to contact my parents and inform them of my "heart condition." *I knew he wanted me to follow up—but to resort to this?*

"I'm fine. Why are you concerned about me? Jason is the one in the hospital."

"Yeah, but you're going through a lot with your mother's health. And you *have* lost a lot of weight."

"I'm good. Don't worry." *I can't believe Armaan called my parents. How dare he!*

"Do you want me to take you to Oklahoma tomorrow? I don't mind. I'd enjoy the time with you."

"That's okay. Dad already offered to give me a ride. I think he needs a break from all this. And my mother—well, you know…"

Mom finished my sentence. "It would be awkward."

I shrugged my shoulders and threw her the quirky smile I bestowed when I was both embarrassed and relieved by her understanding. "Kind of."

That evening Glen, Marian, and their kids hosted me at their house. Marian made her mom's lasagna recipe, knowing it was my favorite, but I barely ate more than a bite. For some reason, my appetite had escaped me lately. Nevertheless, I enjoyed a wonderful evening with their family. Cradling my newest little nephew in my arms relieved me of all my worries that evening. As I gazed into his beautiful eyes, I felt the hope with which newborns grace us.

The next morning, my dad picked me up and we made the ten hour drive to Oklahoma, where my biological mom, Aunt Peggy, and Uncle Bert lived.

My overly suspicious state of mind made the trip uncomfortably quiet. I had now convinced myself that Dr. Rostami had indeed informed my parents of my ECG results. Resenting Armaan for infringing upon my privacy and upsetting my parents, I counterfeited a relaxed attitude, changing the subject every time my father probed. I was so focused on the paranoid conjecture that it never occurred to me that my weight loss, concern for my brother, and the impending death of my biological mom might be why he was worried.

Upon our arrival, Dad greeted Aunt Peggy and Uncle Bert briefly, and then kissed my forehead before asserting a father's intentions one last time. "If you need anything, call me. I can be here that day."

I gave him a tight squeeze and promised, "I will."

Aunt Peggy reassured him. "We'll take good care of her. Don't worry."

Aunt Peggy and I spent the next day at the funeral home. Mother's mental state was too fragile to approach her about her final arrangements. My aunt and I knew that the decision would have to be ours, so we agreed to cremate her, like my brother, Austin, and spread her ashes from a pier on the lake where she grew up. It was the place where she had been happiest and it seemed befitting as her resting place.

Funny how the finality of death changed my perspective: this simple twist of fate released all that baggage I had carried with my mom. The tension between us dissipated as if in a gust of wind, allowing me simply to revel in her presence. Addressing her every whim felt as natural as indulging Michael, Don, or Jean.

For four days, time stood still. I let go and simply connected with my mom. Sometimes I read to her, played music or shared stories about the kids. Other moments we just sat quietly and held hands. Once, I even cradled her in my arms. Through all of this, a peace came over us, restoring our relationship to something it had not been since my youth. For a brief moment, my body granted me freedom from anxiety and paranoia. I forgot all about my problems back home and focused only on this woman whose eyes I shared, and whose problems far outweighed mine.

Then, on my last night in Oklahoma, a horrendous dream woke me up. Images of my daughter, Jean, being hung and tortured terrorized me. A sense of urgency exploded within. I *had* to return home immediately.

Gazing out the airplane window, I searched for Beijing International Airport. The pilot had announced our descent and I was eager to be near my family again. Why did it take so long to taxi? Then there were the passengers ahead of me. *Hurry up!* I screamed internally. *I need to see them!*

At last, I escaped the plane, made it through customs, and retrieved my luggage. There they were, all four of them, standing outside the baggage claim waiting for me.

"Hey, you." Charles grasped my waist with each hand, planting a kiss on me for the whole world to see.

"Wow! I wasn't expecting that," I responded.

"I missed you," he whispered.

"Enough of this nonsense!" Jean barged in, pulling me away from my husband. She did not wish to share Mom with her dad.

Don and Michael stood back. They were used to allowing their little sister first dibs.

I beckoned them over. "Come on, boys. Give your mom a hug!"

And that was that. We were our tight unit again. No anxiety; no foreboding thoughts. I was in my safe bubble.

However, this was only a euphoric moment, my mind's way of allowing mania to trick me. For exhilaration and paranoia are a funny duo. One makes you forget about all your problems, while the other leads you to believe you have ones that, in reality, don't exist. They swirled in my head in such a whirlwind that I could go from jubilation to despair in the blink of an eye.

The magnitude of my problems, both legitimate and fabricated, would soon approach the boiling point, and my bubble was about to pop.

Chapter Five:

Upside-Down Cake

AS KIDS, MY *brother and I entertained ourselves primarily by combining our imaginations and the physical elements around us. In one particular game, "The Wrong Side of the Bed," we gathered supplies needed for our "journey." Lugging non-perishables, Band-Aids, and a can opener, we squirmed into the narrow space between my bed and the wall, a porthole to "outer space."*

Other days we transformed into chemists, sneaking into the kitchen pantry and stealing spices, then mixing them together to create ingenious concoctions. Admitting more innovative than culinary experience, the actual combinations often made us sick.

On the half birthday of my forty-second year, life baked up its own contrivance. An amassment of personal choices and unavoidable events formulated an afflicting recipe, and this time I had not packed accordingly.

Twisting My Kaleidoscope

Recipe for Upside-Down Cake

3 cups motherly love
3 cups parenting responsibilities
2 quarts graduate courses
1 gallon red religious doctrine
1 gallon purple religious doctrine
1 terminally ill parent
1 critically injured brother
1 frightening health condition
1 gigantic misunderstanding
5-7 nights/week sparse sleep

Mix together with fervor for a relatively short time.
Pour into pan.
Listen for popping noises.
Batter will bubble over.
Warning: Watch with care,
might explode in oven.

When finished, taste and adjust for future improvement.

My world was transformed into a mountain I could not envision climbing. I searched for the peak, thinking that if only the top were visible, perhaps I could devise a plan, but the clouds hung low. Faced with my own insufficiency, I considered; perhaps I had reached capacity. Did I really have the tools and strength for so many tasks?

Conflicted, my mind and heart quarreled. One said "Yes," the other "No." Unable to reach an agreement, they searched for neutral ground, but my feet landed in the world of psychosis instead. This gift came disguised, unrecognizable for what it really was. By the time I realized what was happening, Pandora's box had already opened.

Upside-Down Cake

Unlike my other symptoms, Voices was a buddy, a quiet, shy fellow who kind of tiptoed in after the others and observed before making comment. Perhaps it was his way of examining the situation from all angles before offering his own input. When he finally did join in the conversation, his words blended with my thoughts, camouflaging themselves so that it took me awhile to notice him. Once I did, Voices felt so natural, I didn't question his presence, merely accepting and appreciating the companionship.

Isolating myself more and more from those around me, I leaned on Voices for advice and friendship. That friendship turned into romance and thus began a mental affair. Because our relationship was confined to my head, I validated it as a harmless fling. What I didn't consider was how it would affect my behavior.

Meanwhile, language began to twist itself into code. Conversations, books, movies, notes—all spoke between the lines. Nothing was as it seemed and I was left with the arduous task of translating every word that crossed my path—whether written or spoken. Many times, I rearranged language in order to decipher hidden messages. That was probably why Bonnie's email to our Bible study group influenced one of the paths I would explore in this new world I inhabited.

Dear Journeyers,

When I was a child, I was taught that I must always introduce myself when I called someone on the phone. "Hi, Mrs. Garcia, this is Bonnie. May I please speak with Margarita?" Even today, I tell my children to do the same. But to always announce yourself to some people can seem a little silly sometimes. I always chuckle to myself when my mother calls and says, "Hey, honey. This is Mom." All the while I'm thinking, "Yes, I know." I know because I know her voice and because she called me honey, as she has called me for four decades now. I know her voice because we are in a relationship, a long-term, intimate, and real relationship.

Whose voice do you know in your life?

Contemplating Bonnie's message, I realized that I had never given Voices a real name. It was like calling your dog "Dog" or your cat "Cat." I respected him too much for that, so he and I addressed the situation. "I kind of have a name picked out," I explained. "If I tell you, do you promise not to laugh?"

"You know me; I'm your biggest fan."

"Valentino."

"You're kidding me."

"Seriously, I love that name."

"Really?"

"Truly."

"Then nice to meet you, Shannon. I'm Valentino," he replied cordially.

Beaming at our ingenuity, Valentino signed his name at the end of our imaginary contract, cementing our psychotic relationship.

Shannon and Valentino's Contract

We hereby seal this relationship with the following name:
Valentino

Signed,

Valentino
Shannon

Upside-Down Cake

Although my internal companion offered consolation and guidance, paranoia continued to plague me. Everyone acted so strange, even accusatory. At that point, I was convinced that people were indeed listening to my psychotherapy tapes! Otherwise, how would they know so much about my personal business?

In order to find out what was going on, I decided to speak with Dr. Hoi alone as a means to eliminate the taping of our sessions and to protect Jasmine.

> Hi Dr. Hoi,
>
> If you have any free time, may I please schedule an appointment with just you? I want to continue to see Jasmine each Monday. She's warm and approachable and I'm learning a lot from her. However, a private session in the near future would be beneficial.
>
> Shannon

My psychologist replied straightaway, suggesting that just the two of us meet the following Monday.

That afternoon, Bonnie and I ventured out on one of our power walks. Recognizing her as one of the few people who did not presume to judge, I expressed gratitude by disclosing personal information I generally kept to myself. "You know I've been having problems. It's been a tough year."

My friend smiled, accepting my confession as simply life.

So I continued. "But I'm a good person and I'm trying to work things out."

Bonnie's sincere response touched me. "You're strong, Shannon. I'm rooting for you."

"Thanks. The expat community is a bit of a fishbowl—kind of lends itself to gossip. You don't mix yourself in that and I admire you for it." I stopped and looked at her. "I avoid and abhor that kind of unhealthy conversation."

That Sunday, Bonnie walked boldly to the empty spot beside me. Her actions, speaking louder than the preacher's words, blared out, "This is *my friend*" to everyone in the sanctuary. As I was convinced that the rest of the congregation chose to shun me, her mere presence demonstrated in the most powerful way the meaning of a true and loyal friend.

Monday, Dr. Hoi and I discussed the gigantic elephant I wished to shove from the room. Shaken by the arena of rotten vegetables I believed myself to be in, I searched desperately for help and answers in her eyes. Tears clouded my own, despite my attempts to hold them in check.

Dr. Hoi spoke in a soothing tone, embracing my aura in a caring hug of consolation. "You wanted to speak to me alone? Is everything okay with Jasmine?"

"Yes. I like Jasmine very much. It's just that…" Probing the room for hidden ears, I leaned closer and confided, "I think someone's been passing my tapes around."

She glanced toward the cabinet of tapes and then back at me. "Do you think Jasmine did it?"

"No, I didn't want to pull her into the middle of this. You—well, you're a professional. I figured you could handle it."

"Why do you think this, Shannon?"

Upside-Down Cake

"Because people are making statements about things I've never told anyone, except maybe you. They all seem to think I've done something terrible. I haven't done anything to anyone! I make a big effort to be a nice person. How could I have possibly offended everyone?"

"So what do you want, Shannon?"

"I want to put all of this behind me. I want to close this chapter and move on."

"Then consider it sealed."

In an instant, I felt a flash, and the chapter I shut was the one to my sanity. I had officially become a psychotic, in every sense of the word, living on my own planet with Valentino, the voice in my head. I have never been the same since.

The days grew longer and warmer, inviting birds to perch upon each branch of every tree in Beijing. In my state of mind, I assumed they were talking to me. I felt nature's call in everything but dogs. Each time I passed, their barks warned me that a possible bite was attached. Looking back, I assume the scent of insanity attracts some animals, while instilling fear in others.

With only a few days before her summer departure, Adya and I met for sushi next to her clinic. A one-hour lunch break was all we could share until we both returned in August. Her presence filled my surrogate sister's space so well that the prospect of a summer without our philosophical chats dispirited me. However, rather than wasting moments on depressing thoughts, we spent our time updating one another on our plans.

Just like the flash in Dr. Hoi's office, something sparked, tossing Adya's language in the air. As it floated wildly, I struggled to translate her meaning. I feigned routine responses, while the hands of my mind grabbed at her words, rearranging them into one design after another. After we hugged and Adya returned to work, I scooped each configuration into my lunacy bag, determined to make sense of it later.

In an earnest effort to repair the cracked window of our marriage, I arranged a romantic dinner at a little Mom-and-Pop restaurant run by our good friends, Linn and Galvin. Assessing our desires, they dimmed the lights and played tantalizing Italian music in the background so that, at the candlelit table, I regained a brief feeling of normalcy while I gazed into Charles' eyes, giggling sweet nothings and playfully rapping my fingertips against his. Dormant affections stirred within my heart and spirit, kindling a longing that could only be fulfilled in the bedroom. It was a moment we had not shared since my meeting alone with Dr. Hoi.

Valentino seemed to understand our need for privacy and remained quiet. One would have thought this was progress. However, in his absence, a delusion slipped in just as we were leaving.

I recall it went something like this:

"Thanks for the delicious dinner, guys. It was just what the doctor ordered!"

"No problem," Galvin replied. "Our pleasure. By the way, did I tell you what happened to me the other day?"

"What?" Charles asked.

"I found a single diamond ring in the park around the corner. Can you believe it? What luck!"

I glanced at Charles. Panic flooded into me. *This is just a coincidence. It has* nothing *to do with the stone that fell out of my own ring—or is it the same one?*

Upside-Down Cake

Two seconds later, Linn nudged up to me, squeezing my waist and whispering, "The first time I met you, you were so beautiful! I couldn't believe it."

Are you coming on to me? Who are you? What have you done with my friend, Linn? Has the world gone crazy? What the hell is happening here?

Both friends befuddled me. I planned a later discussion with Valentino on this matter. He seemed to be the only one with a level head these days. Thus, I chose to end the evening with the voice in my head, rather than with the man whom I had married.

Chapter Six:

Patience

GRASPING FOR THE air anxiety had stolen from me, I grabbed the Baha'i prayer book Lois had given me. Its words offered comfort and security, making me feel safe. As my hyper-religious state escalated, I relied on the tiny purple volume more and more, and like all other languages, the words popped out and glided, as if prophetic. It became my job to edit and interpret the true meaning of both this doctrine and the Bible.

Sliding into a ritual with the Baha'i prayer book, I convinced Charles to join me. Grasping for any sort of connection, one evening he agreed to read aloud alternately each page from beginning to end. We recited the final words just as the sun rose the next morning.

As exhausting as it must have been, my husband swallowed his pride, adapting to my spiritual fantasies and abrupt behavior, desperate to make things right between us again. Honestly, no one could have made a bigger effort, but he had to wrestle with my irrational state and my fabricated internal lover—a challenging battle.

At some point during that week, Valentino informed me that the world was watching everything I did and reading my thoughts as if I were in a reality television show. I became distraught at the prospect, especially as it affected my children. I also resented Charles deeply for putting me in such a position.

Then, this seductive hallucination proposed marriage, asking me to divorce my husband. Convinced it was part of God's plan, I confronted Charles. Bewildered, he refused my demands.

"I won't do it, Shannon! You're my wife!"

Gazing ahead, I replied softly, "It's no use. I'm already a ghost."

"You're talking crazy, Shannon! Don't do this!"

"Not so loud, Charles. You'll frighten the children."

"The children? Do you not think *this* will alarm them?"

"It's meant to be, Charles. I'll always love you."

And so the conversation continued. We reached a stalemate. I broke his heart. Crushed, Charles lamented, confiding to anyone who would listen. One such person was my psychologist. On my request, he later shared his email with me, along with numerous others.

Dr. Hoi,

My name is Charles. I'm Shannon's husband. I desperately need your help. She started seeing you about two months ago. Since that time, I have seen visible positive changes taking place. Or at least so I thought. Then, last Friday, out of nowhere, Shannon asked for a divorce. It was the worst moment, worst instant of my life. I've tried to talk with her to understand why, but she'll not tell me. She just keeps saying, "I am resolved, you are grasping at a ghost." When I try to talk with her, she stares at me with a blank face, like no one's there. Then, yesterday, she picked me up from work. Within a thirty minute span, I was holding her hand (her way; she wouldn't allow interlocking fingers) and chatting with her.

Patience

She was smiling and laughing. However, we stopped at a restaurant for dinner, and between the time we got out of the car, and into the restaurant, she completely shut down. She'll not look at me, she'll not let me touch her, and she gets visibly upset if I even come close. She even tried to leave before I convinced her that I wouldn't touch her or force her to look at me.

Although we said we would keep this quiet until we worked it out, Shannon's latest shift has now brought our youngest daughter into this. My middle son will also know now. I did convince Shannon to make us a marriage counseling appointment (all before the above episodes). She made one with a Dr. Foster for Wednesday, July 3rd. Shannon said this was the first appointment available. Now, all she'll say is that she'll tell me everything then, that I'll understand, etc. I know from a medical professional perspective, you can't tell me any information, but again, I desperately need your help. Is there a way you can get us an earlier appointment? Can you let me know any information on what I should do, how I should act? We've been married for over nineteen years. Shannon is the only person in my life that until recently I could count on. My heart is ripping.

Thank you for any help you can provide.
Charles

School let out for the summer, and most expat families made their two-month exit. We opted to spend ours in Hawaii rather than return home; but first we waited for my sister-in-law's arrival, as we couldn't wait to see her and show off the beautiful city we had grown to love. With two of my closest friends now gone, Charles reached out to Bonnie, hoping she could talk some sense into me.

> Bonnie,
>
> Hi, I hope your trip is going well. I need to ask a really, really big favor. Shannon and I are not doing well at all these days. We desperately need your prayers to heal our marriage and our lives. I apologize for bothering you with this, but don't know where else to turn. I'm on the cusp of losing the only person I've ever loved and it's killing me inside and out. Shannon will get upset for me asking, but I have to. Say hello to Omar for me.
>
> Thanks,
> Charles

I was so far above the clouds that my head could no longer see the ground below me. It floated from one path to the next in complete disinhibition. Possibly the lack of oxygen at such altitudes forbade clear thinking, but it never occurred to me to question, "Why is this happening?" I simply accepted one bizarre event after another.

Reluctantly, Charles left on a mandatory trip just before Peggy arrived. Grasping any and every thread his fingers could cling to, he showered me with emails, letters, and flowers.

> My Dearest Shannon,
>
> I sit on this airplane completely lost. I have prayed for the past hour straight for God to open our hearts and minds to what is happening now. All I can think of is you, the scent of your hair, your beautiful brown eyes, your delicious lips, your special pug nose, your quirky smirk made by your lips and cheeks, the smell of your

breath, the excitement I get from hearing your voice, the sparkle in your eyes from happiness, the special walk you have, the flicking of your head as you dance, the swagger of your hips as you resonate to the beat of the music. You give me everything and I want to give you everything in return.

I don't know where we or I strayed, but I sincerely apologize for the pain that I've caused you. I sincerely apologize for not listening more. I sincerely apologize for not taking you dancing as I should have. I sincerely apologize for not realizing you.

You, the most wonderful lady this planet has been blessed with. You, the most sincere lady any classroom will see. You, the most devoted mother a husband or child could dream of. You, the best friend anyone could have. You, the most eloquent lady any man could desire. You, my lady, my teacher, my devoted mother, my best friend, my love, my life, my wife for over nineteen years.

It is for all these reasons that I cannot and will not give up on you or on us. I'll take any actions, steps necessary to regain your love. I'll follow you to the ends of the earth if that is what you want. I'll study with you, read with you, dance with you, play with you, sit with you, shop with you, cry with you, scream with you, travel with you. Please just let me know.

I'll be patient as you have asked. I'll give you space as you have asked. But my love for you, my desire for you, my longing for you will never cease, my dearest Shannon.

Love,
Charles

Twisting My Kaleidoscope

And then came more...

My Dearest Shannon,

    Thanks for talking with me last night. I was reading scripture from Baha'i and ran across the below. I firmly believe our marriage is a fortress, our love is a fortress. We have strayed over the past year and for that I'm deeply, deeply sorry. However, I aim to "hold fast" to our marriage as instructed by Baha'u'llah and hope, pray, cry, scream out to GOD, that you will as well.

    Bahá'u'lláh says: "And when He [God] desired to manifest grace and beneficence to men, and to set the world in order, He revealed observances and created laws; among them He established the law of marriage, made it as a fortress for well-being and salvation...He saith, great is His glory: "Enter into wedlock, O people, that ye may bring forth one who will make mention of Me amid My servants. This is My bidding unto you; hold fast to it as an assistance to yourselves" (Bahá'í Prayers, US 2002, p. 118).

    I also found the below on Friendship. It screams you and me. We are truly friends. I have told you over and over again, you are my best friend, my soulmate. You have been there for me when no other was. I want to be there for you for many years to come.

    Friendship: "–[M]an and woman should truly be friends, and should be in sympathy with one another. Their understanding should have a basis in reality–" ('Abdu'l-Bahá, quoted in Agnes Ghaznavi, *Sexuality, Relationships and Spiritual Growth*, p. 121.).

    I hope you have a great day!! I will think about you each and every moment of mine.

I LOVE YOU!!!
Charles

Patience

When my sister-in-law, Cindy, arrived on Chinese soil, she was greeted by Jean, me, and my dear friend Valentino; you might say she found me in full possession of my inhabited guest. Nevertheless, I managed, at first, to arrange my marbles so they at least looked presentable on the outside. However, being the spheres they are, these little round balls never seemed to stay in one place, especially when shaken about, and I was no longer capable of hiding my condition. In just a few short days, my delusion propagated. These creatures have a way of multiplying faster than rabbits. I believed that Cindy, along with a large cult of society, had become obsessed with vampires, so much so, that she and others, in fact, were emulating their behavior.

One day, as we made our way up the Great Wall, I held tightly to Jean, requesting my son Don's assistance in warding off any vampire-like behavior. Loading my daughter into the toboggan that slid from the top of the wall to the bottom of the hill, I entertained sightseers, belting out "Amazing Grace, How Sweet Thy Sound!" over and over again, until we reached the bottom.

"Demonstrate good will, Shannon, it's contagious," Valentino kept telling me, so that's what I did. We made it home safely, and if I didn't turn a few frowns upside down, I must have at least provoked a chuckle or two.

Two days later, Cindy and I made our way to a local market located in a five-story, drab rectangular building. Stalls of clothes, make-up, purses, toys, trinkets, and just about anything one can imagine, were lined up side by side, and row after row. One could easily get lost in the maze of kiosks. Under sane circumstances, I would have introduced Cindy to my favorite vendors, allowing her special purchasing privileges only allotted to their valued and loyal customers. However, on that day, I was under the spell of my internal friend, Valentino, along with a sea of delusions. One such fantasy was that my brother, Austin, was trapped in Hell. His only escape was for me to take his spot, freeing him from his torturous incarceration. Convinced that this was the *true reason* for Cindy's visit, I exhaustively searched behind each stall for clues to his whereabouts.

"Do you know where the jade is? I want to buy a necklace while I'm here," Cindy informed me.

Searching the sign above the escalators, I announced, "Jewelry is on the fourth floor."

We made our way from one stall to the next, purchasing souvenirs and gifts for her to take home. All the while, I believed she was preparing for her reunion with Austin, and as she surveyed the market, I assumed she was actually seeking her long lost mate.

After an hour of searching the building, I became distraught. Where was my brother? Satan made it clear that this was the meeting point. Had I not already agreed to bargain my own soul for his? After all, the wrong sibling was in Hell. Things needed to be made right again. Surely, the time had come. Why could we not find him? What had gone wrong? Suddenly it became apparent. I had not humbled myself enough. I needed to place my body, mind, and spirit in the most humiliating position and beg God to allow this to happen. So, I excused myself to go to the bathroom, found the filthiest stall, and put my face on the floor, imploring the Lord. *I'm ready, God! Grant me this one last wish!*

It never happened. Sure that I had let Cindy and Austin down, I redirected myself to God's other plan: marry Valentino and transcribe His true meaning in all holy doctrines. That's when the danger this stance might impose on my family occurred to me, leading to the delusion that would precipitate my first hospitalization.

I was positive that China's government wanted to kill me before I stirred up too much trouble. Terror struck—axe in hand, it thrashed through my safe bubble, sending me into a frenzy. Urgently wanting to deliver my family from jeopardy, I devised a strategy—arrive at the hospital under the pretext of a physical ailment.

Valentino had informed me that all medical professionals were allies and could be trusted. "Go immediately to Global Care Hospital, if you need a safe place," he suggested. I believed him whole-heartedly—understanding that their staff knew about my predicament and were standing by, ready to evacuate us to the U.S.

And thus my plan commenced.

First, I sent Don for a sleepover with his friend, the son of a U.S. diplomat. Then I arranged for Mr. Peng to make the two-hour drive to retrieve Michael, who was spending the summer with some farmers outside the city. After sorting out the boys, Jean, Cindy, and I would make our way to the shopping center where Adya's clinic was located. All I needed to do was complain of severe stomach cramps and request to see a doctor.

Everything went as arranged, until they sent me to the emergency room. If I could recall more than various faces and sporadic comments, I would, but my mind finally collapsed, heaping the memories of that event into a jumbled mess.

When the physician informed me that they could find nothing wrong, I crumbled, welling up—begging him not to send me home. "They'll kill me if you do," I implored. After further discussion, he determined that I was suffering from severe psychiatric distress and delusions, and admitted me straightaway.

After that, I recall a vague memory that must have been a hallucination, for as she withdrew thick plasma from my veins, I imagined a nurse informing me that I was "not quite ready—winter blood." *What does this mean, Valentino?* I asked. *What am I not ready for? What do you have planned for me?*

After a call to his office from my sister-in-law, Charles arrived. He managed to stay calm and answer questions when I was not able to reply coherently. After a consultation with the psychologist on duty, they rolled me down an empty basement hallway to a room sequestered far from any others. I think it was secured by a special glass door, with restricted access. Charles took Jean home, while Cindy stayed with me for the night.

Dr. Liang, the hospital psychiatrist, arrived with a laptop, presenting a test. Too foggy to question why, but clear enough to accept the challenge, I progressed through the steps of decoding the patterns of shapes and colors. He remarked on his surprise at my success, and then offered a sleeping pill and exited the room.

I remember nothing else until the following morning, when paramedics escorted me to the local psychiatric hospital via ambulance. Shielding my face from onlookers in a sheet, I faded back into my hazy world, where time stood still, until a new doctor greeted me in her white coat at the next location, introducing me to the other patients—my new peers on the wrong side of the bed.

As the only foreigner, I relished meeting the other shut-ins, and connected in particular with three of them. One spoke English, and while she escorted me from one room to the next, she explained where and how we bathed, the cafeteria rules and schedule, indoor and outdoor recreation policies, and where I would sleep. She also introduced me to the other women. Although a bit loquacious, she was friendly. I thought she was the reincarnation of Jesus. Another cried often at first. I recall her sitting on her bed, her head hanging down, shoulders slumped, in obvious desolation. I felt compelled to sit by her side and put my arm around her. One of the girls reported my actions to the nurse. She entered the room and warned me to be careful, and then injected my new friend's arm with medicine.

"She needs to be comforted," I related.

"Yes, you are right, but she also needs medication," the nurse replied.

Internally, I designated my melancholy companion as Mahatma Gandhi's transmigration. Her sadness touched me, and after that, I accompanied her often. Whenever she smiled, it awarded me a cheerful heart.

Patience

However, I grew closest to the third young woman. Mute in the beginning, she made a space for me next to her at the piano as her fingers glided brilliantly over the keys. Her melody moved me, offering a musical tranquilizer to my soul. After that, we shared many conversations. Although she said little, her words spoke selflessly of wisdom. Just before I left, she sketched a picture of me that I kept in her remembrance. In my mind, she was the Dalai Lama.

Men and women were housed separately in two buildings connected by a courtyard and basketball court. Once a day we made our way out for sunshine and exercise. Still manic, my heart raced and I needed my body to move in accordance, so the moment we stepped out the door, I sprinted around the grounds in circles, making it my racetrack. Little by little, other women joined me, and soon we became a herd of mares galloping across our concrete field. They could have laughed and heckled the strange foreigner, as I passed them chatting on their benches. Instead, these women had offered an instant connection and friendship by running alongside me. I have never felt such unopposed camaraderie anywhere before or since.

Even the staff approached me with compassion—I would daresay special treatment. The kitchen crew offered extra food, and somehow discovered that I liked eggs, providing one each morning with my breakfast—an exception to the Chinese-style breakfast served to everyone else. One young woman sat next to me at each meal, encouraging me to eat. I assumed she was the spirit of Mother Theresa.

Other than moments of fear at being locked up and at the mercy of others, I was content in the hospital. Benevolence expressed itself through the words and actions of each doctor, nurse, caregiver, and patient. During one of his visits, I even mentioned to Charles my desire to return as a future visitor. That said, at lunch on my third day, sadness saturated every pore, leaking through my tear ducts, triggered by an innocent query about my children. I simply could not sleep one more night away from them. Their absence felt like a tear in my universe, so, in my "rational state of mind," I made a "composed" request, screaming continuously at the barred exit, "Let me the fuck out!"

Concerned for my safety, the psychologist on duty remained close until Charles arrived. After signing me out, he remembered my pants were still sitting on the couch at home. The ones I wore belonged to the hospital, and I had to relinquish them upon my release. This extremely patient psychiatrist, bearing my hysterical state with poise and tenderness, took off her practitioner's coat and wrapped it around me in order to save my dignity. Refusing to receive medication or intensive counseling, I was no better than before. The slippery slope had only just begun.

Delusions stampeded through every avenue of my mind, crying out to whoever would listen, while terror chased me back and forth. What did they say?

"*The world is watching you for its own entertainment and commercialism!*"

"*Charles is tired of you and wants you dead!*"

"*The U.S. demands your return for its own purposes!*"

"*Your poor children are innocent victims!*"

"*God wants you to use this situation for spiritual purposes.*"

"*You must interpret the hidden meanings in conversations, writing, movies, and music.*"

Such a storm does not decelerate easily. We had not even reached the eye. In a fierce effort to salvage whatever he could, Charles contacted Dr. Hoi.

Patience

Dr. Hoi,

This is Shannon's husband Charles again. I just spoke with Dr. Yang, and she mentioned I needed to send you an email as soon as possible.

Shannon was hospitalized for psychiatric treatment three days ago at University No. Three Hospital. I saw her today, and she insisted on checking out. The doctor on call convinced her to stay, but now I just received a phone call from Shannon, saying that she was checking herself out and that I must come get her. She seemed much better today, but Dr. Yang noted that she should see you as soon as possible, hopefully tomorrow.

Are you available? If you can, please call me.

Hi Charles,

Dr. Yang has updated me on Shannon's condition. I can see her tomorrow afternoon at 1 pm at the Clinic. You may call tomorrow morning at 9 a.m. to confirm this appointment.

In the meantime, if you feel that Shannon is in any way a danger to herself or others, please take her back to the University No. Three hospital and check her in. As the family member responsible for her well-being, you have the authority to sign her in even if she does not wish to stay.

Please reply to this email to let me know if she has

> had a history of hallucinations or delusions, or if this is the first time in her life that she has exhibited these symptoms.

I'm not sure which came first, Dr. Hoi's conciliatory glance toward Charles, or his pleading glimpse in her direction. Either way, an unspoken exchange passed between them before my psychologist approached me with the bluff of an experienced player, pretending to hold the same hand as her opponent.

"I'm glad to see that you're better, Shannon," she began gently.

I pondered before addressing her. *Good. She understands what must be done. Perhaps together we can get through to poor Charles. He's so lost.*

"I am much better. Thank you for noticing. Charles doesn't seem to understand."

Releasing the exasperated breath he'd withheld, Charles responded, "I don't understand what, Shannon?"

"What must be done."

"And what is that, Shannon?" Dr. Hoi slipped in.

"God has called me to serve. If he wants to make things right, Charles will join me."

"Where, Shannon? I don't understand what you're talking about."

"I don't know yet. Wherever God sends us."

"Are you suggesting I quit my job? How will we live? How will we feed and house our children? You aren't thinking straight."

"It's the only way."

"Shannon, I think Charles wants to meet you halfway on this," Dr. Hoi offered. "There are a lot of volunteer opportunities in Beijing. Why don't you start here?"

They don't get it. Valentino, help me explain. How do I arrange the words in their language? My inner friend offered his counsel, guiding the statement unrolling from my tongue. "You see, God has big plans. I don't know what the specifics are yet, but I'm pretty sure AGAS isn't in the picture."

Shock filled my husband's voice. Helplessly, he implored Dr. Hoi to say something—*anything*—to help him out of the box in which I was placing him.

"Shannon," Dr. Hoi leaned closer, relaxing her demeanor to a tranquilizing tone, "why don't you go back to the U.S. first. Get some help. Then when you've had time to consider your plan and all it entails, perhaps you and Charles can come to an amicable solution. Will you promise to do this?"

What do you think, Valentino? Sound reasonable? He offered an agreeable nod.

"Okay."

Thus, fate allowed me one last week in Beijing before insisting I return home. I never contemplated wanting to harm myself or other people. My thoughts were always passive and protective. I never felt suicidal. However, I did think that I might be martyred, although that was not my wish. My aspiration was to demonstrate goodwill and forgiveness, convinced that grace would prevail and open the hearts of others.

After finally accepting the medication issued by my psychiatrist in China, loopiness swirled around my head. I could not tell if the cause was my state of mind or the pills.

Chapter Seven:

Uncommon Senses

THIS SITUATION DEMANDED intensive care for the whole family. Valentino made the delivery. "You *must leave now* for your security, as well as that of Charles and the kids."

As preposterous as his words sounded, they lit a fire under my butt. I needed to board the plane home, and to deliver Charles and our kids into our family's supportive arms. AGAS sent their company nurse, Bria, as my medical attendant. Her primary responsibility was to dispense my medication in a timely manner, so as not to place an out-of-control lunatic on a plane full of apprehensive passengers. She performed her duty well, for I remained calm all the way to the Birmingham hospital.

My parents met us at the airport with the intention of taking the kids home with them so that Charles and Bria could check me into Frank Chasley Hospital. Normalcy insisted on a brief appearance, ordering a lunch gathering before my passage into a community of like minds and their wardens. After finding several restaurants closed, we finally approached a friendly diner that offered a few moments as a family unit before my two-week exile.

Consumed by delusions, hallucinations, and paranoia, I couldn't possibly enjoy a rational discussion with my parents. Even conversations as benign as the weather conveyed hidden messages. As my father commented on the cool drizzly summer, I took it as a complaint on my mood. Valentino told me I had the power to affect the weather—not a desirable outcome for the local community. Eventually, empty plates and unease signaled the hour of departure. Charles, Bria, and I headed to the hospital while my parents took the kids to their house. Too delirious to know better, I awaited eagerly the most painful ten days yet to arrive on my other planet.

At the hospital, Bria watched over me as Charles began the admittance process. An attendant escorted us to an outpatient room to wait, I assume to shield me from others, or maybe the reverse. My two companions leaned silently against the wall, most likely in exhaustion. Meanwhile, I lay flat on a hospital bed. The lull in noise and time offered Valentino and me a moment for our mental chatter and that is when he convinced me that there was a hidden camera in the bathroom where my daughter showered. *How could her father knowingly allow this to happen?* I demanded.

My hallucination shrugged.

Suddenly, I sprang upright and glared at the faultless man across the room from me, screaming, "You dirty, filthy man! Leave my sight!"

Hurt and bewildered, Charles exited. Bria followed, most likely to comfort him.

By myself for the first time in days, weariness overcame me, and I closed my eyes and napped. Meanwhile, Charles returned, this time refusing to leave my side, no matter what. About thirty minutes later, a nurse tapped my shoulder, allowing Charles to say his goodbyes before he led me upstairs to the intensive care psychiatric ward, where I would soon cause more commotion.

After guiding me to my room and introducing me to my bunkmate, the nurse left, giving me time to acclimate and observe my surroundings. My bed sat next to the window, while the other patient slept by the bathroom and door. Two nightstands furnished this otherwise sparse room enclosed by bare walls. A closet in the corner offered a place to hang my clothes and a counter on the back wall gave me a spot to write. However, its sterile appearance and chemical smell felt as inviting as a prison cell.

I walked to the window and peered out, viewing the scenery—the roofline of the building next door and a row of windows that jutted out of the wall adjacent to mine. I spotted a miniature angel hanging on the glass pane of an office across the way. *Did you do that for me? Are you welcoming me?* I wondered at the stranger displaying this tiny figurine. I stared I bit longer. A bird flitted by and landed on the roof below. *Hello friend*, I called out telepathically to the dove. *Please visit me again.* It flew away.

Then I heard her—the frail body on the other bed. She must have been about fifty. Her dark eyes sunk into her chocolate skin and her hair lay matted against her head. Still, a silky complexion, delicate features, and high cheekbones told me that, on a healthier day, she was beautiful. She cried so softly, I could barely hear. I walked over and sat next to her. Feeling the same compassion that overcame me with "Gandhi" in the Chinese hospital, I approached gently. "Are you okay?"

She looked up and smiled. What pretty full lips this woman had. "I'll be fine, honey. I got myself into this mess anyway."

"How?"

My new friend raised her hand up, folded four fingers, and tipped her protruding thumb toward her mouth.

"Alcohol?"

"Yep."

Her eyes switched from a look of remorse to inquisition. "You?"

"They say psychosis." *But we all know the real reason I'm here.*

"Isn't that when you see things and hear voices and shit like that?"

"Yep." *God sent me.*

The attendant barged in. "Ms. Love, you need to get off of Ms. Walker's bed and return to your side of the room," he commanded.

Feeling obliged not to leave her side, I refused.

"Can't you see that this poor woman is in anguish? She needs me," I implored.

"If you don't return to your own side of the room, I'll have to move you physically."

I put my arm over my roommate's shoulder to demonstrate my intentions. He pulled me away immediately and forced me to my bed, explaining that they would restrain me if I continued to make physical contact with the other patients.

The head nurse heard the commotion, entered, and approached me gently, reiterating that, "Up here, there is no touching." His utterances rearranged themselves in the air, landing on my alternative thoughts. Thus, I understood that he, *Jesus,* was pointing out the rules of *Heaven.* For that is whom I certainly thought I was speaking to, and where he had brought me.

Ahhhhh—I see. I smiled graciously and complied. "I understand now. Thank you for explaining."

The coed and noisy environment afforded no access to the outside, driving me even crazier than I was already, while the blaring televisions influenced my delusions. In my state of mind, it felt like torture.

The first four days, fearing that they might be trying to poison me, I spit my pills into the toilet secretly, rather than swallow them. My condition worsened and I became almost mute. With the exception of three people: the head nurse (Jesus), my psychiatrist, and my psychologist, I spoke to no one. However, convinced that everyone could read my thoughts, I continued a dialogue in my mind, and as Valentino slowly vanished, random voices replaced him.

Delusions continued to torment me. I still believed that the world watched every move I made and heard each thought that crossed my mind. I was also sure that I held special powers that could help or hurt people. However, I didn't actually know how to use them. Because of this, I remained on constant guard against another delusion—men all over the world were bidding on me for marriage. They wanted to control my magic. Possibly this was why they raped me mentally—a distressing sensation I felt whenever they came near.

These apparitions continued to accumulate. For although I believed myself to be in Heaven, it felt more like Hell—one that played a devious game for the world to watch. *Surely Charles placed me here to make money*, I convinced myself. As I attempted to break down the rules, I determined that colors and numbers translated into codes and points—leading me to a daily examination of the *Twelve Steps for Alcoholics* poster hanging on the break room wall, which, I was convinced, revealed the rules of the game.

And then there was Charles—who secretly wanted me to die in this competition so that he could take the money and live a life free from me—another figment of my imagination.

If I can manage to stay with him, I told myself—*I won't have to marry anyone else.*

However, my most humiliating delusions—my putrid odor and see-through clothing—dehumanized me. As a defense mechanism, I covered myself with several layers of underwear, shirts, and pants after each shower, which I took incessantly throughout the day. Then it occurred to me. *Why am I making an effort to be presentable? Perhaps I should allow my stench to work for me—as a shield.*

From that point on, I restricted myself to one bath a day. *Ha! Try raping me now!* I mentally taunted the men around me. *I'll spray you like a skunk!*

Apparently, this hallucination had no nose because I continued to feel defiled.

Stuck in a desolate corridor of rooms, bland grey walls restricted me from both nature and color, which I craved. I felt like a caged puma taken from her natural habitat, and I paced the floor constantly, pausing only to gaze out the hallway window at the tree below. I imagined myself sitting beneath it, reading a book. If only they would allow me that—

Sometimes, I plopped myself on the floor and admired the sparse paintings hanging on the hall walls, studying the lines and hues of each, speculating on their messages. However, I yearned for more—a way to express myself—an avenue to investigate these crazy thoughts racing through my head, so I approached a nurse, requesting a pen and paper. She offered me children's markers instead.

Frenziedly, I interpreted passages from my Bible and Baha'i prayer book, wrote pacifistic strategies to champion world peace, and scribed inspiring notes to myself. After each furor, I made my way to the nurses' desk, requesting strips of scotch tape. With my ten fingers holding as many pieces as they could carry, I returned to my room to hang my thoughts on the wall. Before long, papers covered my living quarters. Adding to the disarray, I refused to surrender my clothes to the hospital staff, washing them by hand in the bathroom sink and hanging them anywhere I could find space.

Then there were the pictures of my children. Missing them terribly, I placed their photos on the bare spots that my wet laundry and erratic scrawls did not cover. The clutter must have agitated the cleaning staff, but they never complained. However, once, a psychiatrist deadpanned while perusing the wreckage, "You know, Shannon, less is more."

Although Valentino's presence became more and more rare, I had not forgotten him, and one day I thought I might even have met him in physical form. It happened when a young therapist lectured during a group session. A strange sensation enveloped me, making my whole body hot and tingly. Thinking he might be the hallucination I fell in love with, I asked, "Are you him? Why do I feel this way?"

No stranger to madness, he replied considerately. "I'm just a twenty-seven year-old social worker. But I think you'll figure it all out."

Over time, my mania subsided and eventually, I took the papers down from my wall. Organizing them neatly in stacks, I placed my work in the nightstand drawer to pull out and review daily. I also began to join in group therapy regularly—and pop out more than five words a day—a huge feat for me.

After ten days in intensive care, the doctors finally transferred me downstairs to the acute psychiatric department. I gathered my things, placing them in the bag provided by an attendant and followed *Jesus,* all the while speculating that he might be tricking me into going somewhere even more dreadful than *Heaven.* However, I made it safely to the less intensive ward, where I spent the next five days. This time, my destination was a pleasant surprise.

A large lobby, furnished with a television, tables, chairs, games, and crafts, was squeezed between two courtyards—one indoor— one outdoor. My eyes chased the aperture to the outside. I blinked to reassure myself that I was indeed gazing upon a waterfall that streamed into a fishpond shaded by two beautiful trees with a colorful flower bed as a finishing touch—an oasis. Nature— sunshine—vitamin D. It was what I desired more intensely than anything—and there it was—the place I would spend every free moment for the remainder of my stay.

Jesus caught the slight lift in the curve of my mouth. "Why, Ms. Love," he hooted. I believe that's the first time I've seen you smile."

I beamed at the man who had gone the extra mile to extend good will. *Thanks, Jesus. Thank you for bringing me here.*

Although my psychosis persisted, I began to communicate a little with other patients and self-enforced attendance in group therapy sessions, art being my favorite. Painting and listening to music helped me recover my lost joy and always ended too soon. Other treatments, such as games and discussions, had their place, but I was still too antisocial to enjoy them. However, one therapist forced me to recall and reflect upon unpleasant memories in a safe and accepting way. She helped.

Unfortunately, one stubborn delusion persisted in haunting me throughout my psychotic break: mental rape. Consequently, the presence of men disquieted me, and as much as I tried to separate myself from them, they always seemed to make their way to my table, their kind and non-threatening manner a moot effort. I asked a nurse for tampons. Wearing them assured me that I was protected somehow. I continued to use them for over a week after I left the hospital.

After my hospital stay, I returned to my parents' home with some residual social anxiety. Being around more than two or three people was more than I could handle. This even applied to family. Recognizing my discomfort, they allowed me to reacclimatize gradually.

I began five days of outpatient therapy the following Monday. The 9:00-3:00 schedule offered an easy routine. At first, I was the most tight-lipped one in the group, but I became more social as the week progressed. The all-female sessions benefited my disposition. One day, I spontaneously wrote something that I admired about each outpatient, and it helped remind me of the social creature I am. Slowly, my delusions began to fade and my eyes opened to reality. One evening my mom brought out my wedding video, an ingenious act that led to a turning point. I hadn't seen it in years and agreed to watch it with Charles, a man I still did not trust.

My eyes fixated on the television screen as I studied carefully the twenty-three year-old face of the man sitting next to me, looking into the eyes of my younger self—vowing to honor and cherish his bride—trembling hands—quivering voice. Yes, this youthful Charles appeared nervous, but there was something else I saw in his face. Could it be tenderness? Could it be love? I turned to examine the middle-aged Charles as he watched the video. His eyes were red.

They looked sad, defeated. *Hmm.* I considered. *At least at one time, this guy truly loved me. Could I have misjudged him?* That moment caused me to second-guess the way I had been thinking. I chewed on the thought, digesting it slowly, and then later that week, I chose to believe that his love was sincere.

My willingness finally to listen to him with an open mind allowed my husband to help me see how bizarre my thoughts and actions had been. I believed him more and more each day and the delusions finally left me.

Chapter Eight:

Amazing Grace

WHEN I WAS in second grade, a young Japanese woman, Ms. Sasaki, a first-time teacher, bestowed her approving smiles on my class. Her beauty, youth, and energy won the hearts of every seven- and eight-year-old in the room, including mine. I admired her so much that I longed to be part Japanese, just like her. Once I even linked my short, black hair with her heritage. I was too young and naive to recognize Ms. Sasaki's restrained laugh at my assertion.

One of her stories took place when she herself was a little girl living in Japan. Her traditional home had many ceremonial decorations called *washi*, delicate wood-framed windows of thin translucent paper that required meticulous care. However, like all children, my teacher, who wore mischievous gloves from time to time, simply could not restrain herself from poking tiny perfect holes through the *washi*, leaving her seven-year-old eyes to face the frustrated ones her mother wore at the scene of the crime.

Perhaps not as precious, although I consider all life to be so, my spirit felt much like the *washi* at the end of my three-week hospitalization. Fragile wood framed my frail interior and the tiniest little poke could leave holes where the previous ones had sealed themselves.

Hence, I was capable of travel, but had to take care not to relapse. We returned home.

"Ling" my Caller ID informed me as my phone rang two days after our arrival back in Beijing. I was torn by mixed emotions. One shouted, "Yay! Ling! I missed you," while a second whispered, "Are you ready to face everyone?" However, Courage wrapped her arms around me in reassurance. "This is your friend. She's calling because she cares. Take a chance. Answer it." I did.

"Hey," Ling chirped.

"Hey. How's it going?"

"Good, but I'm calling to check on you. How are you doing?"

Warmth blanketed my heart. *I'm so fortunate to have such wonderful friends.* "I'm much better. Thanks for calling while I was in the hospital. I'm sorry I didn't say much—it meant a lot to me."

"No problem. Listen, I spoke with Bonnie and Adya. If you're up to it, I'd like to have all of you over for lunch one day this week. We've been thinking about you and thought it might be easier to meet at my house—something quiet, simple. Then you can leave if you feel…" She paused…"well, overwhelmed."

"That actually sounds really nice. How about tomorrow?"

"Tomorrow it is!"

The ease that only appears when one is surrounded by friends who care genuinely, with no agenda other than their concern for you, pervaded our lunch date. I recounted the summer events, answered questions, and in return listened to their own vacation events. It felt like the most normal conversation I had enjoyed in several months, and amazingly, that was just what I needed.

Amazing Grace

I stared through the window of our Buick GLE, the standard vehicle for expat families living in Beijing. Smog remained bashful today, and a vague outline of the mountains garnished the city's backdrop. I glanced at my watch: 10:45. "Mr. Peng, will you please drive faster? I don't want to be late."

He shook his head. "Traffic, Madam." Lingering at 60 km/hr in the middle lane, cars passed us on both sides. Mr. Peng was known as AGAS' safest driver. He refused to ruin his perfect record because *Tai Tai* could not leave the house in a timely manner. Even so, he threw a tender glance in the mirror. He worried about me, as did everyone else.

My phone vibrated, announcing another text from Charles. "Good luck! Be strong! I love you!" This past summer had traumatized him most, because while I was delusional, he'd known what was happening. I understood with complete clarity and appreciated my husband more than ever. That was why I was in the car, agreeing to his employer's terms of allowing us to return to China for a few months to provide the closure we needed.

Dr. Hoi had returned to the U.S. and recommended an old student of hers who had moved to town recently. Given my medical records, I suspected this new psychologist anticipated facing a wild-eyed lunatic, so I wanted to make a good impression. Above all, my goal was to act sane.

At the Wellspring Clinic, I waited in a comfortable lounge chair. A cappuccino maker next to a hot water dispenser and a selection of teas offered a pleasant welcome. The coffee table in front of me hosted both Chinese and English magazines. The staff seemed engaging and cheerful.

"Shannon?" I turned my head. A tall, dark haired man stood before me, smiling warmly.

"Dr. Attar?"

"I'm no doctor. Please call me Dabir. May I show you to my office?"

I followed him to a room with a small desk and an assortment of couches and chairs arranged in a square, with no additional ornamentation. Observing my surroundings, I waited for my therapist to select a seat before choosing my own. I wanted to place myself as far from him as possible.

"I apologize for the lack of decoration. I just moved here from California and am in the process of making my second home—well—a home." He paused.

"I suppose you know why I'm here," I said matter-of-factly.

"I understand you went on a pretty wild ride this summer. Would you like to tell me about it?"

He didn't flinch. Yep. This was a California boy. Time to lay it all on the table.

"I'm recovering from a psychotic break. I was first hospitalized in Beijing in June. Then my husband's employer, AGAS, evacuated me to the U.S. for an additional three weeks in an intensive psychiatric care unit. They require that I attend individual counseling three times a week and couples counseling once a week. My case manager requested I write a brief summary of my experience to give you."

"May I see it?"

As I handed him the paper, embarrassment burned my cheeks. "I thought I would be giving this to a woman."

Dabir read my story while I scrutinized his face. His unruffled expression impressed me. "Tampons. Very clever. I wouldn't have thought of that."

"Bipolar I, with psychotic features, that's my official diagnosis."

"People who are bipolar have a unique way of thinking. They see things from a different perspective than the rest of us. Look at Jesse Jackson, Jr. and how he's contributed to society. Historians and psychologists now believe that Thomas Jefferson and Vincent van Gogh were also bipolar."

"I'm taking two prescriptions: Depakote as a mood stabilizer and Latuda as an antipsychotic."

"Do they work for you?"

"I would probably still be psychotic if it weren't for the Latuda. I'm not sure about the Depakote. I've never been a moody person. Those closest to me might describe me as slightly manic, but mild-tempered otherwise."

"You appear quite calm now."

"Can you see me three times a week? If not, I have to leave China."

"I'm sorry. I thought we had already established that."

"My psychotic history doesn't frighten you?"

"I worked with an organization that specifically treated psychosis patients in California. Although the stigma may discourage some mental health professionals, I see it for what it is."

"What is that?"

"The brain's way of making sense of a reality that doesn't?"

"When can we begin?"

Attending to dinner, I reflected on the day. Ayi Ju should have left already, but continued to linger. Like everyone else, she worried.

"Go home, Ayi."

A stern look of determination accompanied her shaking head, "Much work."

I understood she felt remorse for leaving me home alone when I was sick. She'd returned to the house each day, trying to get in, but I had met this poor woman at the door with one reason or another not to let her enter.

My bizarre behavior and dress unsettled her, my entire body covered in loose, dark clothing with wild curls adorning my head. I wore only the slightest bit of make-up and barely spoke to anyone, locking myself in the bedroom for hours. The vivacious, well-groomed brunette she knew had disappeared. It was as if someone else had taken over my body, and I'm sure it scared the hell out of Ayi Ju.

Now, Ayi kept herself busy with excuses to stay, and she bided her time until Charles returned home.

I wrapped my arm around her. "The kids are here. Go home and rest."

Ayi piddled around a bit more. When she could think of nothing else to keep her, she reluctantly straddled her scooter and left.

I turned on my iPod and continued cooking. Music soothed me and preparing dinner made me feel useful. I needed so much to *give*—especially to Charles and the kids. After the storm I had created for them, I had to find a way to restore the normalcy we once had. Providing a home-cooked meal felt comforting. It was a start.

Cooking also afforded an opportunity to be alone and think, while giving the appearance of sanity. I wasn't sure if I would ever truly return to my old self. Perhaps, once the road system of the brain suffered an earthquake, something different replaced it. Still dealing with the aftershocks, I could not yet predict what that might be.

"Mom? Do you need help?"

"Hi Don. I didn't see you."

"You were in your own world again. Are you okay?"

"I'm fine, honey. I was just focusing on dinner. It's been awhile since I've cooked. Are you hungry?"

"Yeah, what're you making?"

"Chicken enchiladas, your favorite."

"Thanks. Will Dad be home soon?"

"He left the office an hour ago."

Making an entrance as only Michael could, my older son sauntered through the door and kissed me on the cheek. "Something smells good! Enchiladas?"

"Yep. How was school? Were they okay with you arriving a few days late? I spoke to the guidance counselor to explain the situation. You know, he would be a good person for you to talk to."

"I don't need to talk to anyone, Mom. I'm fine."

"May I at least make all three of you an appointment with my therapist? What you went through with me was difficult. It may help to speak to someone."

"Mom, you keep asking and we continue to tell you that we're fine. Please leave us alone about this!" Michael demanded.

"I love you so much—and know what I put you through."

Don piped in. "It's okay. You were sick. We understand."

The boys rolled their eyes at one another, chanting in as if on cue. "We love you, Mom."

I knew it wasn't okay. The problem was how well they understood. I let it go for the moment. Everyone's eyes were only on me and I could not divert them elsewhere.

The slamming of the front door and shuffling of feet announced that Charles had arrived. Before, he detoured each evening to unwind at the computer, but that was the old Charles. Tonight and every other night since we'd returned home, he searched for me the minute he walked in. He needed the reassurance that I was here in every sense of the word.

Tender hugs and kisses became our new evening greeting. "Dinner smells delicious, but you should've let Ayi cook. You need your rest."

"I *am* well rested and I wanted to cook for my family."

Charles frowned. "Dabir said that you should take it easy."

"I *am* taking it easy. Ayi will not allow me to do anything around the house. I *needed* to do this."

"You're the boss."

I pinched him on the bottom and winked. "Ha! Ayi's the boss!"

Jean walked in, grinning. To see her parents flirtatious and playful again mollified her even more than Mom's enchiladas.

As the largest international hospital in the city, Beijing Global Care kept offices in many buildings and sections throughout town. One such building, within walking distance of Charles' office, was the place where we had our marriage counseling with Dr. Brian Yang, a highly respected clinical psychologist known for his warmth and exemplary skills at working with families.

We walked in hand-in-hand and announced our arrival. A few minutes later, a tall, slender, well-dressed man introduced himself as Brian and led us to his office.

"I hear you had a difficult summer."

Charles spoke first. "You could say that."

Brian looked at me. "And how are you, Shannon? What can I do to help?"

I squeezed Charles' hand. "You can focus on Charles. I've received an incredible amount of support and get individual counseling three times a week. However, this experience was equally traumatic for Charles—perhaps even more so. He's had to be the rock."

"You have wonderful insight, Shannon. Most people don't realize how much this sort of thing affects the whole family. Thank you for acknowledging it." He glanced at Charles. "Would you agree? How has this influenced you?"

Stifling a sob, Charles wiped his reddening eyes. "You see, Shannon and I've been together since we were seventeen. When I lost my eye in a football accident, she was the only one to stick by my side. She called me every day and visited me as often as she could. She became—my world."

Brian replied gently, "And you felt like that 'world' had been taken away from you."

"Yes, Shannon is—" This time, tears washed his flushed cheeks. "Well—she's my everything."

Brian looked at me. "Do you hear him, Shannon?"
"Yes. I know that now. I didn't before."

"Exhibit A."
Before taking a seat, I presented evidence for Dabir's inspection.
"The paint on your nails suggests that a bit of art therapy was in order this morning."
"You could say that."
"That statement attaches to a story," he deduced.
"Yep."
"Then make yourself comfortable and deliver me a 'once upon a time'."
"You recall that hyper-religiosity played a major role in my break."
"Yes."
"Well, vampires somehow stitched their way into the theme."
"Carry on."
"I believed that Hollywood had ignited an international vampire obsession. And a large sect of people adopted the practice of drinking blood, black magic, and sadism."
"You mentioned this in our first session."
"Another pervasive thought was of an impending Armageddon."
"And what was your role to be?"
"I functioned to enlighten people, to affirm the world of an opposite and equal reaction—that the Garden of Eden would once again open its gates."
"Literally?"
"Figuratively, manifesting itself as world peace and ecological restoration."
"So—what does this have to do with the paint on your nails?"

"Don, my middle son, bore the brunt of my delusion."

"Shannon, you're quite gifted at confusing me."

"I have many starting points, but don't worry. They all end at the same place."

"Then please get them to the finish line before our hour expires."

Targeting Dabir with a peevish gaze, I continued.

"As I was saying, I designated Don as my collaborator. Convinced that the vampires had bewitched him in retaliation, I rushed into his bedroom one morning singing, 'Hush Little Baby' over and over again to break the spell."

"I'm sure he loved that."

"He hated it. That's why he locked his door when I went to the bathroom."

"And you saw this as a sign of revolt."

"In the extreme! Horror took over my body and placed a hammer in my hand."

"Figuratively."

"Literally! Fearing that he would climb out the bedroom window and leap to his death, I grabbed a hammer and broke the handle of his door—along with the wood around it."

"—and somehow this leads to your painted nails."

Grinning. "I repaired the door this morning."

"You certainly know how to make a short story long, Shannon."

"Yep."

Charles and I found our spots on Brian's *love* seat.

Our counselor spoke first. "Last week, Shannon, you said you asked Charles for a divorce. I understand that this was part of your psychosis, but it had to stem from something. What do you think that was?"

I looked at the ceiling to ponder the origins. "I suppose it started with my heart condition."

"You mean the health concerns and testing you went through last year?"

"Yeah, I was really scared and tried to tell Charles, but he just rolled his eyes and dismissed it. So I joked about it and eventually withdrew."

Brian looked at Charles. "Is this true?"

Charles nodded his head, and then focused on me. "You're right, Shannon. I didn't pay attention to your feelings, but *you know* I'm not good at reading people. Next time, *please scream*! Shake me! Do whatever it takes to make me listen!"

I understood then that it was as much my fault as his. "You're right. I should've been more assertive." And at that moment, I promised myself that I would, for both of our sakes.

In the business of family, I could boast that Love Incorporated operated for nineteen years as a well-oiled machine. Marrying young, Charles and I unfolded in unison as we grew into adulthood. Our blank canvas permitted nature to brush our roles into a design that most suited us.

Charles, our CFO, crunched, distributed, invested, and forecast numbers as well as anyone I have ever known. He mastered when and how to spread our dough so that bread always filled our baskets. He was and still is a capable and generous provider.

As CEO, I managed the other half, allocating duties, organizing family social functions, handling supply chain management, administering basic healthcare needs, and moderating our home temperament. I wore my title with honor and felt gratified by its yield.

So, when psychosis punched our family in the belly so brutally by taking me out, it essentially kidnapped the executive director! My magic carpet ride left them without a rug to set their feet upon and our family institution sustained monumental shock. Thus, when the bounty was paid, they greeted my release with uncertainty.

I was concerned that my oldest son, Michael, had lost his comfortable shoes and replaced them with a meeker pair. At fifteen, his age aggravated matters. High school politics, search for identity, and physical metamorphosis present enough problems, but my Michael carried another burden—that of a crazy mom.

Although his words spelled, "I*M**F*I*N*E**M*O*M," his actions screamed otherwise. The boy who once filled his social calendar weeks in advance now remained homebound. His leadership roles and afterschool activities diminished, and so did his grades. My son was suffering and although my eyes peered through a curious lens, they weren't blind.

Dabir perused my mood survey. "Your 'anxiety' and 'worry' windows rank higher than usual."

"It's Michael. He hasn't been himself since we returned home. I think he's depressed."

"Can you give me some examples?"

Shame held my eyes down as I outlined his behavior changes.

"You didn't ask for this to happen, Shannon."

"Neither did Michael."

"Why do you beat yourself up?"

"As a therapist, *you know* the effect an unstable mother has on her child."

"How long have you been a mom, Shannon?"

"Almost sixteen years."

"How would you rate yourself before you got sick?"

"Not perfect, but I offered as much love and support as any good parent."

"Then why are you judging yourself on only one inch out of a foot and a half?"

"Because it severed the bond."

"That's a cognitive distortion. Please rephrase."

"Okay, the bond is still intact—but the edges have unraveled."

"Give them time to repair themselves."

"You aren't a mom! You don't understand!"

Dabir paused for a beat. "What if you had suffered a heart attack instead, Shannon?"

"That's different."

"Why?"

"Because it doesn't elicit bizarre behavior."

"That's because disease attacked an organ that performs a different function in the body."

"What are you saying, Dabir?"

"I'm trying to show you that you blame yourself because illness struck one anatomical system, when you would not if it were any other."

"I never thought of it that way."

Brian leaned back in his chair, as if preparing himself to hear a story. "Shannon, I recall you mentioning something in our first session. You said that you didn't realize that you were Charles' world before your break, but now you do. Will you expound on that?"

"Well, when I was psychotic, I thought Charles was out to get me. In my eyes, he was a monster, and I treated him as such, pushing him away every time he tried to get near. However, he refused to leave my side. He visited me every day at the hospital, bringing me cards, gifts, anything I asked for, no matter how badly I treated him. Those kinds of actions must only come from unconditional love. I've never tested him like that before. So I didn't know."

Charles grabbed both of my hands, staring firmly in my eyes. "Now do you understand?"

"Yes, baby, I understand."

Dabir sighed. "You carry a lot of guilt."

I coughed up my usual response, "Wouldn't you?"

"How does this feeling benefit you?"

"It keeps me on my meds, for one."

These conversations generally led to Dabir's "cognitive distortion" speech.

I waited, but he pursued a different approach.

"I'm giving you homework tonight."

I grinned. "Gee, thanks."

"I want you to think of something you gained from this experience—not your family—just you."

That evening, while painting with my daughter, it came to me.

Sometimes convolution mutates into something spectacular. Despite gnarling my joints and antagonizing my emotions, psychosis did offer one treasure: a sixth sense, a special lens elusive to the mainstream eye.

Although my eyes absorbed a fractured reflection, they also examined the dazzling patterns that converted with each twist of my head. Every angle of any given situation presented itself to me. It was as if I saw the world through a kaleidoscope. Was it a curse or a blessing? I suspected a bit of each.

Dabir inspected the two books in his lap. "One is much heavier than the other. Does it hold more weight with you?"

I focused on the Bible I had handed him. "More history."

"And what does that equate to?"

"Well, it's part of my heritage."

"So you feel a certain loyalty."

Reclining, eyes directed inwards, I considered a reply.

"It's kind of my Michael."

"I'm perplexed, Shannon. Are you insinuating that Christianity is your first-born?"

"Sort of."

"Please expound before you lose me."

"Sibling rivalry makes a place in my home as much as anyone's. As reassurance, I tell my children that each is my favorite. Jean holds the cherished position as my youngest. I designate Don as my beloved middle, and treasure Michael as the first."

"So Christianity is your treasured first?"

"Yeah."

"And in what order does the Baha'i faith fall?"

"I suppose my cherished youngest."

Dabir twiddled the thumbs of a man uneasy in his approach. "Is this why you jumped in the pool last summer—with all your clothes on?"

The chuckle within me bounced from my belly, up my esophagus, and pried open tight lips for release. "I still can't believe I did that!"

Dabir's giggle played along. "It could've been worse."

"It was the community pool!"

Laughter's tears filled my eyes as I added, "You're right, though—at least I didn't take them off!"

Composed once again, Dabir inquired. "Why did you do it?"

"I thought I was meant to baptize myself publicly—to make a statement."

Contorting his face to lasso that rowdy snicker into submission, my therapist summed up. "An official cleansing."

Brian's *love* seat had now become quite cozy for Charles and me, and sharing intimate details about our marriage with him seemed as comfortable as the couch.

"Has all this changed the dynamics of your relationship?"

"A lot!" I exclaimed.

Charles chimed in. "Yeah. Pretty much everything is different."

"Like what?" Brian queried.

"First of all," Charles replied, "I used to be a workaholic."

"Now he's home by six-thirty every night," I finished his sentence.

"I'm also much closer to the kids. I've had to be. Shannon always took the main role with them, but she needs my help." He smiled. "I think that's a good thing."

"We're more open with one another," I added. "I used to keep my feelings and thoughts to myself."

Brian looked at Charles. "And what about you?"

Charles considered his reply before remarking, "I'm a little gun shy—hypersensitive, if you will. I kind of walk on eggshells, afraid I'll spin her into another break if I don't."

The pit in my stomach began to sink. "I'm so sorry, Charles. I don't want you to feel that way."

"I know you don't. But I do."

I texted Charles: "Here."

My phone vibrated. "On phone—be down soon."

"Maybe ten minutes, Mr. Peng. Should we pull up to allow other cars through?"

Mr. Peng moved forward to a less congested area in front of

Charles' office, located in the center of Beijing's Central Business District, adjacent to the CCTV tower or "the pants," as many of the locals called it.

After years of listening to clients' conversations, I supposed Mr. Peng was the keeper of much personal information. I think he found our family endearing. He and Charles were pals, sharing thoughts and requesting advice from one another. They hashed over attractive cars and women, never letting the car get too quiet.

I usually buried myself in a book as he chauffeured me from one place to the next, but his bad days never escaped me. "Are you not feeling well, Mr. Peng? Do you need to go to the doctor? I can catch a taxi," I would insist. Some nights, when he carted the kids around, he joined our family for dinner.

Charles continued his daily pattern, struggling to leave the office most days. Although his responsibilities were immense, communicating with offices from many time zones, he loved his job.

Now, sliding the door open, my husband slipped into the seat next to me, another change. Before, he rode up front with Mr. Peng, the two men leading the chariot. Since our return to Beijing, he took his place next to his lady.

"You look nice."
"Thank you. So do you."
"Does everyone know where to go?"
"Yep."
"How many people?"
"Eighteen."
"Are you nervous?"
"I'm excited—looking forward to it."

To celebrate my recovery, new beginnings, and the care and support of genuine friends, I arranged a dinner in 798, Beijing's art district. Some pals of mine had just opened a new restaurant and this was my oasis. I often joked that it could be my home if only my talent equaled its aspirations!

Arriving fashionably late, Charles and I were the last to enter—and we both lit up as we found ourselves surrounded by cherished Beijing companions. Wishing to demonstrate our appreciation toward those who embraced us through a disquieting time, we each made our way around the room to greet these very special guests with warm hugs and handshakes.

Charles surprised me by decorating the place with balloons and flowers. A large bouquet that decorated the center of the appetizer table caught my eye. When I commented on how exquisite it was, my husband informed me that he was not responsible for that particular piece and pointed to Ling. Apparently, she had collected money from all who attended in order to purchase it.

After dinner, the owners granted me permission to give everyone a tour of the restaurant—a real treat, as it was constructed from an old three-story factory and doubled as an art studio and their home. My personal favorite was the bathroom. To enter, we climbed a ladder, pressed a button, and waited for the door to elevate to an open position.

We laughed, shared stories, and made toasts. Overall, the evening maintained a jubilant air. However, Charles did shed a few tears toward the end when he confessed to the weight of the load this past year had placed on our shoulders and thanked everyone for helping us carry it.

My alter ego replicated that night carefully in oil. It hangs magnificently in the back of my mind so that I may gaze upon it from time to time when loneliness takes over.

Chapter Nine:

Release

MY RELATIONSHIP WITH Dabir deepened and he became a cherished friend. I felt an ease with him that previously I had limited to those of my own gender. Later, I would discover my transference of feelings for my late brother, Austin. For now, he was a like mind. We both seemed to view life similarly and dialogue was easy. We even shared the same taste in literature. The kinship assuaged me.

Unfortunately, as satisfaction with my relationships mended, the effects of my medication took a toll. For the first time in my life, I felt real depression. It hit hardest each evening, about an hour after taking my pills. Brusque illusions of death's release flashed through my head. Steadfast, I used every tool Dabir provided. However, when my hands began to tremor, I surrendered. In the absence of an American psychiatrist (necessary for American pharmaceuticals), I arranged an appointment with my physician.

Well aware of both my physical and mental medical history, Dr. Rostami's resources were limited nonetheless.

"You look well Shannon—better than the last time I saw you."

I got straight to the point. "I've been very sick."

My doctor's eyes softened. "Adya told me. I'm so sorry you had to go through all that." Then his face changed to something that looked like remorse. "I've lost some sleep since our last consultation."

"The ECG. Yeah, sorry. I didn't react so well, did I?"

"*I* didn't realize your state of mind. Otherwise—"

I looked my friend straight in the eyes to demonstrate my earnest intentions. "*Please* don't worry. *No one* had any idea what was going on with me, not even me."

"But I'm afraid I aggravated your problems."

"How? By being concerned?"

"By being *overly* concerned."

"Please understand my sincerity when I tell you that your compassion is what makes you such an amazing physician. If anything, you helped. After all, you're the first person who recognized *and* pointed out my need for psychiatric help. *Believe me* when I say things could have been much worse for me under the care of another doctor."

"You're too kind, Shannon."

"And you're an excellent physician, who did your job well, Armaan."

Resolved, we moved on to medical matters.

"So, shall we return to business then? Let's begin with your ECG. In light of the severity of your anxiety, combined with all the tests I put you through last fall, we can determine that your heart is healthy. Just promise me that you'll see a cardiologist for a check-up once a year."

"I promise. But that's actually not why I'm here."

"Oh? Then how can I help you?"

"It's my Latuda."

"Your antipsychotic?"

"Yeah, it makes me feel depressed."

Dr. Rostami frowned. "I'm not a psychiatrist, Shannon."

"I know, but there aren't any from America here. I'm at a loss what to do."

"Aren't you returning to the U.S. in two months?"
I didn't like where this was going.
"Can't you hang on till then?"
"Can't you switch me to another drug?" I pleaded.

He shook his head. "Sorry. China doesn't use the same pharmaceuticals as the States."

"I don't know if I can tolerate this till December."

"I'm afraid if you don't, you'll be playing with fire."

Feeling defeated, my flame burned low, cowering back from the gaping abyss. Just before my charred wick fell cold, I berated myself, slapping sense back into me. *Look at yourself! Can you not see? You have reached an impasse. Will you continue this spiral downward, leaving yourself debilitated, unable to mother your children and face your upcoming repatriation? Listen to your body! Respond accordingly!*

So I did. Scribbling my plan on paper, I delivered it to Dabir the following day:

Release

Dabir inquired simply. "Talk to me."

"It's my medication. It incarcerates me."

"So—?"

"I'm titrating myself off. No one is listening to me. The meds make me *feel bad*. If something that is meant to make me feel better has the opposite effect, it isn't doing its job."

Dabir bit his nails. I knew him well enough to recognize his apprehension.

"I was nervous about telling you. I want to do this safely. Someone needs to know—to help me monitor. I don't want to relapse."

Witnessing the resolution in my eyes, he conceded. "Then let's do this right. Make me a list of your behaviors *before* you became psychotic."

"Anxiety—then mania. You already know this."

"I want specific behaviors and symptoms—for example, you mentioned extreme weight loss."

"I can do that."

"And write a letter, giving me permission to contact Charles if you show symptoms. You're a stubborn woman."

"I know. Thanks, Dabir."

A few weeks later, I had successfully titrated myself off all my medications, and was able to hide the fact from Charles by pretending to take the pills. I became quite effective at simulating the evening ritual. When my energy and outlook picked up without any negative symptoms, I knew that I had duped everyone and resumed control of my life.

Bashfulness flushed Brian's cheeks as he contemplated his approach to the subject some therapists thrived on. "I'm not suggesting anything, but this happens to be an important part of a healthy marriage. How is your—hm—hm—romantic life?"

Careful not to read too much into his meaning, I digested his words while Charles looked anywhere but at our faces. "You're talking about sex—right?" I asked.

Feeling completely at ease with the subject both male participants seemed to tiptoe around, I took it upon myself to delve into the topic. "Charles and I have always done quite well in the bedroom. It's actually where we seemed to click the most."

With his face beet red, Brian attempted to remain low key. "Did that change with your break?"

Release

Forgetting his embarrassment, Charles piped up, "You bet it did!"

"Yeah," I admitted. "When I was manic, my insatiable appetite escalated until it was much higher than Charles'. Hyper-sexuality seems to be one of my symptoms during that phase, but then, shortly after I became psychotic, it dropped to zero, and I became abstinent. So now I'd like to say I'm at a good level—above average in the libido realm—but not out of control."

Soothed by being taken out of the hot seat, Charles agreed. "I think that, romantically, things are back to normal with us, which was the better part of our relationship to begin with."

Brian dug a bit more. "Shannon, was there anything that helped your intimate side return?"

"Yeah, time, feeling safe, and steamy romance novels."

"Please take me home, Mr. Peng."

My driver must have wondered if Madam's mind had taken another leave of absence, for his rearview mirror reflected a woman entranced. Sagacity tilted my head and attention toward the gold loop on my left hand.

Unknowingly, Dabir had treaded on thin ice that afternoon when he made the most innocent of comments.

"You're playing with your wedding band. It must be quite special to you."

"Actually, it was my grandmother's. I wear it to remind me of her," I mumbled before changing the subject quickly. Otherwise, the conversation would lead to me confessing a crime so heinous, I could not bear disclosing it even to the man who held my diary.

When Madness had entered my temple the previous summer, carrying a hamper of dung, ignorance shut my eyes to the mess he would make. Yet he did, slinging crap in every corner, cackling at his mischievousness. Like many undesirable guests, he refused to clean up before departing, leaving *me* with a pile of dirty laundry.

My *real* wedding ring fell into that pile and like a needle in a haystack, I could not get it back, because just before my medical evacuation, I flushed it down a toilet at the local market, convinced it was cursed with black magic.

This splinter twisted deep into Charles' heart, and I could still see it bleeding from time to time.

Chapter Ten:

Adieux

DABIR LOOKED AT me. "You move back to the U.S. in four weeks."

"I know."

"I'm sad."

"I will be too, when the time arrives."

"Not yet?"

"I prefer to savor each moment until the day of departure. Then I'll fall apart."

"You aren't one to waste time, are you?"

"I wrote a poem for Charles."

Dabir perked up. "Really?"

"It's about our travels, life overseas, and our return home."

"May I see it?"

He had a way of making me feel proud. "Here."

Love Undertaking

Fleeing our haven
Abandoning our sanctuary
Forsaking our atoll
Our desire
Our aspiration
Our destiny!
Thirsting for enterprise
Yearning for quest
Relishing exploit
Skimming, skirring, sweeping us to other worlds
Unbarring our eyes
Exposing our minds
Disclosing our ears
Allowing spirits
To enrapture our souls
Longing to be seduced by their enticements
Cherishing perception expansion
Blending our thoughts
Creating a cyclone
Petrous storms reshaping us
Spawning glorious works of art
Within
A synthesis only attainable
By leaving
Embarking on a feat
Only confronted
By the tenacious
Ultimately
Returning home
Allowing our tongues
To divulge
The marvels
We have discovered

Adieux

"Well, what do you think?"

"I like it. Excellent attitude. Have you given it to him yet?"

"Yes."

"And—?"

"I think it made him feel appreciated. That was what I wanted to convey. I wanted to thank him for our adventures."

"And now he knows."

"Now he knows."

Snuggling up on Adya's couch, I breathed in, savoring the scent of her Ayi's *jiaozi*, filled with veggies and cheese. Adya served the Chinese dumplings and salad for lunch during my Tuesday visits.

I rubbed my hand against the denim surface of her couch. The ridges caressed my palm. Avan, her five-year-old, sat on the floor next to me, leaning over the coffee table, gluing assorted plastic pellets into a mosaic design while chanting a song he had learned in school. So bright, this young man was.

Then Caspar's chubby little feet toddled up to me. "Hannon! Hannon! Ook at meeee!"

He bent over, dropped his head onto the floor, and attempted to roll forward. His body, not quite cooperating, meandered sideways.

I clapped my hands. "Yay, Caspar! You did it!"

Glowing, he propped himself up, puffing out his adorable chubby cheeks. "I id it! I id it!"

All at once my heart sank. This was my second home. Adya, Roberto, Avan, and Caspar were my family. I couldn't take Adya's dumplings, their snug denim sofa, or the people with me. I was leaving my sister behind, and unlike with those residing in the U.S., I could not guarantee an annual visit.

Nope! I shook myself out of it, refusing to brood. *I won't do this.*

However, as sisters often are, Adya's mind and mine were on the same page.

"You can't abandon me," she commanded.

"Move to Houston with me," I coaxed. "You're an incredible doctor. Any practice would be lucky to grab you."

Adya shook her head. "China is our home now."

"Will you stay here indefinitely?"

"I can't predict the future, but if I can get through the winters, we want to stay and bring our kids up here."

"The winters—they're hard for you."

Adya's face fell. "I don't know how I'll make it through this next one without you. I'm just not a cold weather person. I *need* sunlight. At least *you* take my mind off of those dreary days."

"I won't miss December and January," I admitted. "But you're strong—one of the most courageous people I know. And if it gets to be too much, move to a warmer part of China."

Adya shifted on her side of the sofa to make room for Caspar. He hopped up and snuggled into her side before she changed the subject. "And you. Are you going to be alright with this move?"

"I'll be okay."

She compressed her lips, blowing a frustrated sigh through her nose. "You know how I feel."

"I know."

"You're stable and thriving here. Why couldn't they let you stay until June? How does it benefit you or your family to pull your kids out of school in the middle of the year?"

"Because, under the circumstances, AGAS was being quite considerate to allow us to return at all; they only did this to give us closure."

Adya shook her head. "I don't buy it."

"That's because you're with me. You see how well I'm doing. All AGAS knows is that I was so sick that I had to be evacuated and hospitalized for several weeks. They probably feel that they took a big risk bringing me back at all."

"You're too generous—but I suppose you're right."

Our bittersweet last session with Brian took place in early December, a few weeks before we left. He would soon return to California to spend the holidays with his family and Charles needed to use the time traveling to AGAS' various offices around China to say his goodbyes. However, today, our farewell and gratitude would be extended to Brian, the anointed healer of our marriage.

"I'm going to miss you two," Brian confessed.

"We're going to miss you, Brian. I can't thank you enough for all that you've done for us," I replied.

Humble as always, Brian responded, "I was only a facilitator. You made it happen. As a couple and a family unit, it's obvious how strong you are."

It was Charles' turn to express appreciation. "But your rose-colored glasses helped us see it. Thanks, man."

Then Brian returned to business. "We should probably discuss your move. How're you going to make it work?"

"In the past, Shannon has pretty much taken care of it all," Charles confessed. "This time, I'm going to have to help."

"And how are you going to do that?"

"It'll be tricky. I have a lot of traveling to do these last few weeks, but I'll do as much as I can on the weekends."

Brian glanced at me. "Does that work for you, Shannon?"

"Yeah, I actually feel quite strong, nothing like I did back in October. I think I'm ready. Plus, AGAS will send a moving company to pack everything up for us. The most arduous job will be our inventory list."

Brian laughed. "I remember that, moving here. My wife put sticky notes everywhere to help mark which category to *place* each item in on the list."

Charles chuckled. "Hey, as often as we've moved, you still give us a new idea. Thanks!"

"You're very welcome."

The conversation lightened from that point on. We finished with a hug, even between the two guys. Brian was a crucial part of our healing process and we would never forget him for that.

Counseling three days a week mixed with three kids and a move kept me busy and I had not seen Ling in awhile. I missed her and called. She made time for me the next day at one of our favorite local Chinese restaurants, the Brown Door. Anyone unaware of its excellent food would walk in, survey the bare walls with their peeling paint and the concrete slab floor that looked dirty no matter how often they scrubbed it, and then leave *this dump*. However, along with other expats, we understood that we'd be amply rewarded with enticing delicacies of local cuisine.

"Are you ready for your big move?" Ling asked.

"I'm getting there—doing a little at a time."

"What have you done so far?"

"You know: sorting, getting rid of stuff, looking at houses and cars over the internet, etcetera, etcetera."

Ling squeezed her shoulders together and twirled her hair. This was how she always introduced good news. "You remember Scott, my younger son?"

"How can I forget? He's a doll!"

"Well, he graduates from Rice in May."

I squealed, leaning over the table to hug my friend. "Congratulations! You must be so proud."

Adieux

"Yeah, he's a great kid. Both of my boys are."

"Kids? Those boys are men now!"

She winked at me. "Yep, but they'll always be my babies. Anyway, what I was thinking is that Rice is in Houston. You'll be living there by then and—"

"Of course you can stay with me! I wouldn't have it any other way."

"Thanks. I'll have the weekend free to spend with you. We can have some girl time."

"I'm thrilled! It will give me something to look forward to."

"Speaking of school," my friend inquired, "will you start back once you get settled?"

I crossed my legs, interlocking my fingers in introspection. "I've thought about it. But…"

"But what?"

"Well—a guidance counselor. Would anyone want to hire a psychotic to work with kids?"

Ling rolled her eyes. "You're only a psychotic when you're symptomatic, Shannon. I haven't seen you display any lately. Plus, I think your experience would help you relate better to kids with mental illness." She leaned back and crossed her arms. "I actually think it could work in your favor."

"Thanks. Brian and Dabir said the same thing—guess I just need to get my nerve up."

Ling had given me something to consider. Becoming a guidance counselor was a dream I had given up, but maybe I shouldn't just yet.

"How does your family back home feel about your return to the U.S.?" Dabir questioned.

"They're happy to have us nearby again."

"But they won't be in the same state."

"No, but at least they won't have to go halfway around the world to get to us."

"That's true. Will you be in the same time zone?"

"Yep."

"Do you think they'll visit?"

"I think they'll try. It should be easier."

"How do *you* feel about this?"

"That's the best part of moving back—and the most difficult about being away."

"A happy reunion."

"Yeah, we'll spend the first two weeks in our hometown—return to our roots—encourage the kids to participate in the Christmas rituals Charles and I grew up with."

"Quite different from your typical holiday vacation."

"Yep. No more exotic December excursions—at least for awhile."

"Are you disappointed?"

"I'm anxious."

"Why is that?"

"Because the last time I saw everyone, I was out of my mind."

"You're talking about your parents."

"My parents, brothers, sisters-in-law, cousins—*everyone*."

"And you're not sure how they'll react."

"Exactly."

Placing his hand on his chin, my therapist crossed his legs and studied me, as if he were fixated upon a work of art, contemplating its meaning.

"May I tell you what I see when I look at the woman sitting across from me?"

"Sure, why not?"

"I see a strong, intelligent, level-headed person who would find great difficulty convincing anyone that she's out of her mind."

Adieux

Sometimes Dabir astounded me with his archery skills. This was one of them, hitting the target and scattering my insecurities into oblivion.

"Thanks, Dabir."

Please Join Us
in
Wishing a Bon Voyage
to
The Love Family
Where: The Krueger Family Home
When: 12:30
Sunday, December 14, 2013
RSVP: Bonnie and Omar Krueger

"Don't forget the luncheon at Bonnie and Omar's place tomorrow," I reminded Charles. "The kids are invited."

"Who all will be there?" Charles asked, glancing over the invitation.

"Adya, Ling, and their families. I asked Bonnie to keep it small."

"There won't be any kids Don's and Michael's ages."

"I know, but Omar and Bonnie went to a lot of trouble to do this. They bought gifts for all three of them."

Charles grinned. "You get to tell the boys then."

Usually we had to force Don and Michael to attend social functions with us, but this time was different. The Krueger family had been particularly kind to them, and although they were teenagers and often more interested in their own peer group, they thought a great deal of our neighbors. Plus, Bonnie was a fantastic cook and the boys generally didn't turn down good food!

The next day after church, we headed straight to Bonnie's house. She had slipped out early to finish preparing everything before we arrived. Aromas of sweet potato casserole and pot roast whiffed through my nostrils even before I went through the front door. I walked in to see both her dining and kitchen tables already set, and in the corner of her living room lay a display of gift bags. My dear friend had obviously awakened before dawn to prepare for this meal.

After lunch, we gathered in their living room for a special "ceremony." Bonnie and Omar took turns presenting each of our kids with an exclusive gift from Beijing, unique to his or her personality, along with a short speech describing what made each of our three children special. They also bestowed three crystal globes imported from the U.S. that must have taken two months of prior planning to arrive on time. I breathed in their generosity, recognizing that Bonnie and Omar were not only part of our Beijing family, they were treasured companions for life, and I whispered a quiet *thank you* in the air, for no one's ears but my own.

My eyes bounced from the letter on the computer screen to the piles of files and books on the floor, then to the stack of papers piled before me. "Do you want to review the inventory list?"

Charles thumbed through with meticulousness only he possesses. "What're you writing?"

"It's a letter to Dabir. Will you read it and tell me what you think?"

I stood up and gave Charles my seat.

Dear Dabir,

I recall our first meeting. Could I actually cultivate a trusting, intimate relationship with my therapist—especially a man? I was skeptical. Your energy and enthusiasm, combined with your unflinching response to the mess placed in your lap, revealed your vision of the human behind my psychotic mask. I left your office with hope that perhaps we could make this work.

Our sessions began. You figured me out quickly, recognizing my need for reciprocation. Revealing bits and pieces of yourself gave me confidence to divulge. Little by little, I shed my armor and allowed you to nurture and educate me. As our relationship grew, a new concern plagued me. Was I becoming too dependent? Was my vulnerability too raw? Frightened of the pain of revealing my most concealed thoughts and emotions only to shut the door soon after, I began to wonder. Confidence in my strength to promote such a relationship that would come to an abrupt end wavered. You reassured me that my newly-acquired tools would help when the time approached. It's here.

Am I ready? These are things I know:

You taught me how to mold my pile of shit into a sturdy structure. Many professionals sculpt something that looks pretty on the surface. Mine also functions well. Its proper heating and cooling afford a balanced climate. The sensitive security system recognizes when to summon reinforcements. Its firm foundation withstands massive storms.

You provided a safe place for me to go for help after recovering from the most difficult experience of my adult life. Access to such a retreat is a treasure.

I'm a better person for knowing you. You exposed me to an amazing man. Being the deeply caring person you are, unafraid to be true to yourself and what you believe in, while also respecting perspectives other than your own, made my life richer.

Saying goodbye to you will be painful. As you said, "It's the part that stinks!" I'll grieve the loss of a dear friend. You cannot contribute to someone's life as you have to mine and be considered anything less. It doesn't seem like enough. But the best words our language provides for this sort of thing are, "Thank you."

With Warmest Wishes, Deepest Gratitude, and Some Sadness,

Shannon

A few days later, after bundling into my heavy coat and winter boots, I informed the moving crew that I would return home soon and walked to a local pizza joint around the corner. Dabir had arranged to meet me there for our final session, in consideration of my time constraints.

The morning's hectic schedule shielded me until I slid into the seat, facing my therapist. Suddenly, the hourglass dropped its last grain of sand into my heart, weighing it down with a heaviness that signifies the end of a meritorious time and friendship. I picked at my food and did my best to carry on a conversation; however, somberness colored my mood and encased the tone.

We arranged a final few Skype sessions over the holidays. Nevertheless, I knew that this was the last time I would see him in person. We embraced in farewell and I said goodbye to my brother—for, in my heart, that is what he had become.

"Happy anniversary, babe." Charles and I united our champagne glasses along with a gentle kiss in the business class seats to honor

Adieux

twenty years of marriage. This would have to be the extent of our celebration, for it fell on the bittersweet day we left China. Our Beijing family, Ayi Ju, Mr. Peng, and Steven (our relief driver) accompanied us to the airport that morning. As loved ones generally do, they watched until we could no longer be seen on the horizon, and we held on to the images of their smiling faces as we crossed it.

The clouds carried us from a six-year journey abroad back to our mother tongue. Thankful for the memories, the transition of one season to the next arrived with mixed emotions. Repatriation unfolds itself in such complexity. It manifests an unpredictable outcome, especially for children. Jean, Don, and Michael might very well feel like foreigners in their own country.

We weren't quite sure what to expect. We understood that life in China—and Angola before that—had changed us. The world shrank before our eyes, and our family and culture consisted of a vast wardrobe of shades and textures we did not yet own when we left the first time.

Psychosis introduced us to yet another world. While its turmoil certainly entangled the fabric of our clan, it also added cohesiveness. We emerged a tenacious crew that had fashioned a unique design.

Migrating through extrinsic and intrinsic pilgrimages forever transformed us as individuals and as a unit. The Love family would set foot on American soil in shoes far different from those in which we left.

Chapter Eleven:

Doors

STEPPING OUT OF the elevator on the fourth floor, my feet forced their resistant body to a door at the end of the hall: 404. A gentleman exiting moved aside as I made my way in reluctantly. My allegiance to Dabir, combined with sheer therapeutic burnout, tempered my enthusiasm for inaugurating a relationship with the person who would soon invite me to echo a story already disclosed.

A tall, smartly dressed brunette greeted me.

Soft lighting and warm couches bedecked with fluffy pillows and cozy blankets were commingled with art, inspirational plaques, various trinkets, and family photos. Evidently, Dr. Marsha Russo contrived a marriage of playfulness and serenity in her design.

Still, I withheld myself, looking her in the eye impassively.

Dr. Russo broke the ice. "All the way from China, huh? What was that like?"

"It was hard to leave," I replied stiffly.

Ignoring my frigidity, she countered enthusiastically. "And now you're back in the good old U.S.A. How's that going?"

"Remarkably smoothly. I forgot how friendly everyone is here," I answered, omitting the warmth my comment implied.

Unruffled, she held my information sheet. "I see you have kids. How are they adapting?"

"The younger two made friends straightaway. My oldest is taking longer to find his place."

My psychologist paused. "So, you tangoed with a hurricane last summer?"

There was no hesitation in my reply. "If you're referring to my psychotic break, yes."

"Will you tell me about it?"

Once again, I recounted each month of my new calendar, beginning in May, two years prior.

A tender smile crossed the face before me. "Dabir sounds quite special. I'm not sure I can fill his shoes."

"He understands me."

"In what way?"

"When you were a child, did your teacher ever present you with a color-by-number page?"

"Yes."

"Equate each of your clients with a number on that paper, symbolizing the color you use to fill the spaces. After successfully deciphering the code, you have a complete picture."

"So what color are you?"

"I'm the arc up in the corner with all the numbers."

"A rainbow."

"A lot of color—more than most therapists want to deal with."

Dr. Russo didn't fit Dabir's mold. Lamenting my loss, I simply saw her as "not him."

Climbing into my car, I checked my phone. There was a text from Charles. "Call me."

I closed the door and turned on the heater. Houston's winter was a bit cooler than I expected. I dialed.

"Hi. This is Charles."

"Hi, babe. It's me, calling you back."

"Just wanted to see how your appointment went."

I sighed. "Marsha's nice."

"But?"

"I don't know. Dabir was so cool. I could talk to him about anything without shocking him."

"Give her time. I bet you'll feel that way about her too, soon."

"I'm not sure. She looks young, but she talked about her grandkids."

"So?"

"So that means she's old."

"Well, there you have it then."

"What do you mean?"

"If she's old, then you have nothing to worry about."

"Huh?"

"Think about it, Shannon. She's a psychologist with a lot of years under her belt. She's probably already heard it all."

Two weeks later, Marsha's own unique shape won me over. Mirroring many of my past life encounters, she exemplified that different does not necessarily mean better—or worse. It simply offers a new point of reference.

"Tell me more about your break," Marsha encouraged. "You said you heard voices."

"I really only heard one voice until I was admitted into the Birmingham hospital."

"Birmingham, England?"

I chuckled. "No, Birmingham, Alabama."

"I wasn't sure, since you were overseas. Last week, you only mentioned that they evacuated you. You didn't really say where."

"Oh, yeah, sorry. I've told my story so many times, I forget what details people do and do not know."

"That's okay. So, did this voice speak to you often?"

"Yes. He was my confidant. I named him Valentino. Around the time I entered the psych ward in Beijing, I wouldn't make a move without consulting him."

"So you were completely dependent on him?"

"You could say that."

"Did he taunt you or ask you to do dangerous things?"

"No, he actually told me to be careful not to do anything that would cause me physical harm. It was as if he was afraid that I might."

"But he did tell you to swap places with your brother in Hell. That doesn't sound good for you."

I shifted in my seat. "It's complicated. Valentino didn't ask me to do that. I *wanted* to. I thought that Austin had been taken there wrongly. The only way to free him was to go in his place."

"But then the injustice would have been directed toward *you*."

"Of the two of us, Austin was the better person." I closed my eyes before looking at her again. "Besides, it was only a delusion."

My psychologist clasped her hands together as if in prayer and tapped her knuckles against her mouth gently. At first, I thought I had stumped her. Then she spoke, making it apparent that she was the one directing this conversation. "I think you feel a lot of guilt about your brother's death, Shannon. Why is that?"

I hesitated. No one had ever asked me this question, and although I knew the answer, she caught me off guard.

So, directing my eyes slightly to the left of hers, I replied, "Because things were always easier for me than for him. Yet, he was actually a much sweeter person than I was. Then Austin died at thirty-six. It doesn't seem fair—and don't say life's not fair. I already know that."

"Shannon, tell me something. How was Austin's life going before he passed away?"

"Things were great. He and his wife, Cindy, had just returned from a trip to Hawaii."

"Didn't he have a heart attack?"

"Yes, he was on military duty in Puerto Rico, and then fell over in the hotel lobby where he was staying. It all happened suddenly—so quickly that the paramedics could do nothing for him by the time they arrived.

Marsha leaned her head sideways, as if to determine from which angle to approach me. "Have you ever thought that maybe he was the lucky one?"

"What do you mean?"

"Well, you said that he died quickly, with little or no pain, at a high point in his life."

I wasn't quite sure how to receive this. "How is *that* lucky?"

She beat her chest, directing my attention to *whom* she was referring. "He gets to skip old age—and *that* ain't for sissies."

Laughing now, I replied, "Point well made."

Charles and I cuddled in our bed. As I could not stay awake until midnight and he couldn't force his eyes shut at nine-thirty, my husband had fallen into a routine of lying down with me each evening just before I went to sleep. Some nights we conversed and on others, he just held me, depending on how exhausted we each were. This evening I wanted to talk.

"I miss my friends."

Charles brushed my hair with his hand. "You have Ollie and Rebecca just down the road. That's why we moved to this neighborhood, to be near them."

He was right. Ollie and Rebecca were two of my closest girlfriends from Angola, who happened to be transferred to Houston shortly before us. Ollie's husband worked for AGAS, not so surprising. However, being South African, Rebecca's move was pure good fortune. Still, I had grown attached to Adya, Ling, and Bonnie and grieved their absence.

This nomadic lifestyle scattered our friends around the world, offering a more intimate relationship with our planet. However, it also left our hearts aching, longing for those we left behind in various places.

"I know. Rebecca and Ollie keep me from being lost—I just wish I could have brought my Beijing girlfriends with me."

"Think about the kids, Shannon; they have no one. This is a completely new playing field for them."

He was right. Here I was, feeling sorry for myself, when Michael, Don, and Jean had managed to wake up every morning prepared to face uncharted territory. At least I had two dear friends at my backdoor, and although Houston is a large city, spanning many miles, my family chose to live where Mom would be happiest. I was a lucky woman. Charles had a way of putting things in perspective for me and I appreciated him for it.

I nestled silently, my back against his chest, and grabbed his hand to kiss his knuckles, deliberating how I would approach him with the next subject: my biological mom.

She had survived her poor kidney function, despite experiencing another stroke. The extra time allotted to her allowed the dynamics of our relationship to change. Now we functioned as a true mother and daughter unit for the first time in years. Unfortunately, because of our move, my shortened holiday vacation did not permit an opportunity to see her.

Flipping my body over and wrapping my arms around Charles, I voiced my intention. "I want to fly to Oklahoma next weekend to see Mother Jones."

Charles twirled my hair through his fingers. "Are you up for it? You just made an international move."

"Yeah. Aunt Peggy and Uncle Bert will take good care of me. Don't worry."

He continued playing with my strands in silence. Acknowledging that my husband needed time to think, I waited.

"I guess you could leave Thursday morning, after you get Jean off to school, and I can work from home Friday," he suggested finally.

I squeezed the man who indulged my every whim. "Thanks, baby. You're the best!"

When I arrived in Oklahoma, my mom's condition had deteriorated since our last visit. Still, she hung on and smiled when she saw me. Aunt Peggy commented on her upswing in mood whenever I was around. Seeing her again also offered me a sense of peace. The second chance fate offered both of us truly was a blessing.

I took advantage of every minute we had together, and asked her to share stories of her past, such as her happiest moment, funniest experience, most embarrassing encounter, and the thing she was most proud of (other than Austin and me). In return, I updated her on our move and the latest family news. You could say we came to know one another a little better.

Time flew by, and after four short days, I returned to Houston and the arms of Charles and the kids—consoled, refreshed, and feeling a little more settled in my new home.

My relationship with my psychologist had improved exponentially, and I no longer felt ill at ease about disclosing to her. That said, she still must have sensed a slight reservation on my part, because on this day, Marsha delved into an inquisition about my other therapist, possibly to offer her insight on how to approach me most effectively.

"Tell me more about Dabir, Shannon. Was his approach similar to mine?"

I shook my head. "No, he was a huge advocate of CBT. You know, he helped me take negative and distorted thoughts and restate them."

"Did it help?"

"It did a lot with the shame and guilt I felt. I mean—I made a complete fool of myself, and traumatized my family."

"You seem to still hold on to some of those hostile beliefs about yourself."

"They slip under my skin sometimes, but Dabir pointed out the physiological roots of my mental illness. He helped me recognize that the affliction was the bad guy, not me."

"Did he also clarify that *anyone* suffering from the same hallucinations and delusions as you would probably have behaved in a similar way—possibly worse?"

"Yeah, he did a pretty awesome job with that."

"You're lucky. Dabir sounds like an extraordinary counselor. This disease has such a stigma attached to it. Even people in our field sometimes have a difficult time relating."

I smiled. "Dabir was special."

A *knowing* expression crossed Marsha's face. "How do you feel about him?"

"I told you. He has become a significant person in my life."

"Do you find him attractive?"

Oh! I realized now where she was going. "Dabir is a handsome man, but it's not what you think."

"It's okay if you had some erotic feelings toward him. It's not an uncommon experience for clients."

I shook my head adamantly. "No! It's not like that at all—trust me. Dabir was like my brother."

"Like *a* brother or like one of your *particular* brothers?"

"Actually, he reminded me of Austin, and we shared the same ease in conversation I had with my brother. It felt good to talk to someone who thinks like I do."

Marsha paused before asking her next question. "Have you ever heard of 'transference,' Shannon?"

"Dr. Hoi brought it up once. Isn't that when you visualize

someone as another person, and consequently share the same relationship?"

"It's something like that. This may have happened with you and Dabir."

I leaned back in my chair, allowing the idea to digest. "You know, that's probably why it was so hard to say goodbye. I had already done it once, when Austin died. Here I was going through another separation with Dabir, in December."

The following evening Adya called me. At first I thought Charles had emailed, informing her I was lonely, but when she delivered her news, I knew otherwise.

"How are things in Beijing?" I asked.

"Cold! But not as bad as last year."

"That's a relief. Last winter was miserable. How are Roberto and the boys?"

"Good. I have something to tell you."

"You're pregnant!"

Adya huffed. "Sometimes I wish you wouldn't complete my sentences. But, yes!"

I was ecstatic. I knew that Adya and Roberto had wanted a third child and that this was wonderful news for them. "I'm so happy for you! How far along are you? Do you feel sick?"

"So far I feel great, but I'm only six weeks. You, my mom, and my gynecologist are the only people who know other than Roberto."

"That truly is great news! When is the baby due? I want to visit you after he's born."

"September. I really hope you do. We'll give you the best room in the house."

We gabbed on and on about her pregnancy details, possible names for the baby, and how she would handle maternity leave. Then Adya suggested an idea she had been toying with, one that would lead to my next big life decision.

"You know, Shannon, I've been thinking about something for awhile now."

"I should move back to Beijing?" I teased.

"That would be fabulous. But seriously, I was thinking you could write a book."

"A book?"

"Yeah, about psychosis and your experience."

"And how did you arrive at that?"

"Well, you love to write and I think you could help a lot of people this way."

Hmm. My friend had captured my attention. "You've given me something to consider."

Adya sparked a desire within me that had lain dormant since my break. *A book. What a concept.* It could be my avenue, my contribution to society. I liked it. I would bring the idea up with Charles and the kids, and if they offered their support, it would be the extra push I needed to get the ball rolling.

Marsha had been my psychologist for a month now and had grown into a loveable character. Her dress, slender figure, bright face, and long dark hair painted anything but an old lady picture in my mind. Yet, she had not quite acquired the "cool" factor Dabir carried. Today, she would earn that honor.

"In our last session, you mentioned that when you were in the hospital, you heard voices other than the initial one, Valentino."

"Only in the Birmingham hospital," I corrected.

"Were they friendly, like Valentino?"

"Mostly. They kind of joked around with me. The hospital was such an intense experience. Maybe they were a way to lighten my mood."

"Were they male voices?"

"Not all of them. Some were men and others were women." I smirked. "Funny thing—they all had different accents."

Marsha chuckled, and then moved on. "Did you have any visual hallucinations?"

"Only once that I'm sure of. Do you recall my sensation of being mentally raped?"

"You haven't told me about that yet, but go on."

"I thought it was a means to impregnate me. One day as I lay in my hospital bed with terrible stomach cramps, I assumed they were labor pains. After they relented, I stood up, looked out the window, and saw a bright red circle in the sky. It began to propagate all over the horizon. I assumed then that the circles were little baby stars that I had birthed."

"Hmm," Marsha replied.

"Crazy, huh?"

She shook her head. "It's not that. I was just thinking about an experience I had back in college that might resonate with yours."

My eyes popped. "You had a psychotic experience?"

"Sort of," she explained, "I tried LSD once and I think it manifested itself in the same way."

That's it! She got it! Marsha truly understood. Now, I could make it clear for her. "So imagine someone spiking your coffee with LSD every morning for two months."

"Wow!"

"That's psychosis."

For three months now I had been lying to Charles about taking my medication and my conscience was getting to me. I made an appointment with Dr. Hallow, a local psychiatrist. I had my agenda set: He would see how stable I was and "officially" take me off the Latuda. Instead, when I arrived, he responded with skepticism.

"Psychosis is a physiological problem, Shannon. You can't just 'will' it away."

"My circumstances are different than most," I retorted. "I've only had one break and it didn't occur until my forties."

We went around and around for over an hour, until I finally admitted that I could not be certain this would never happen again.

"What *will* you do if you have another psychotic break, Shannon. What if your husband leaves you next time?"

Ha! I have him here. He has no idea how much my Charles loves me. I looked my psychiatrist square in the eyes. "My husband will *never* leave me."

In the end, I convinced Dr. Hallow to consent to an official discharge from medication, under the condition that I agreed to keep a bottle of Latuda in my cabinet in case I became symptomatic. He also demanded that I call him immediately if that occurred. Although we came to a consensus, our personalities clashed. I didn't like him and vowed to myself never to return.

Chapter Twelve:

Encore

AS I'VE SAID, I'm not a numbers person. I tend to avoid assigning exact measurements and instead just approximate when, how much, or how long things will be. Aware of the less utilized part of my brain, I had begun working Sudoku puzzles as a cognitive exercise. Sometimes I place one last number in the box, only to discover that I missed something along the way, so that I have to retrace my steps to solve what I already thought I completed.

This happened soon after we moved to Houston. Having made an international move, settled our children in school, and shaped our house into a home successfully, I confidently declared myself out of the woods.

"You're moving to Chicago. That's near your parents, right? Are you excited, or is it too close to home?" I asked Bonnie.

She had Skyped me first thing that morning to share the news.

"I'm delighted. They're getting older and I've missed them a ton from over here."

"Are you sad to leave Beijing? What about the kids and school?"

"We love it here. You know that. Still, I'm homesick, and ready to be near my family again. I am nervous about repatriating the kids. That's what I wanted to talk to you about. How have yours adjusted?"

"Jean and Don made friends the first week. It took Michael a little longer. He's older and has pretty much established himself as a third-culture guy—he has a more difficult time relating to some of the kids here."

"Mine are all Jean's age and younger."

"They should be fine then. Jean had been away since she was four, and she's already reciting the Pledge of Allegiance and singing the national anthem."

Bonnie laughed. "Mine have it down from their scout troops."

We continued on about the kids, her move, Omar's and Charles' jobs, and life in general. Then Bonnie asked me about my plans to return to graduate school.

"I've changed directions."

"Where are you going, my friend?" she inquired.

"I'm writing a book about my psychotic experience."

Bonnie's face fell slightly before returning my sentiment. "I applaud you, but *please* be careful."

"Why? I'm writing a book, not climbing Mount Everest."

Bonnie hesitated. "Shannon, you're my dear friend and I support you. I actually think you'd make an amazing author and you have a story worth telling." She lapsed again. "It's just that—well—reliving all that again might be difficult for you—it could cause you to relapse."

"It might also be therapeutic."

"That too," she admitted. "Just be careful, okay?"

"I will."

"I love you, Shannon."

"I love you too, Bonnie."

Encore

Right around that time, AGAS' service team notified Charles that the shipment that carried our furniture, paintings, linens, and kitchen supplies from China had arrived in Houston, and would be delivered to us in a week. Since the move, we had been living with rental furniture, plastic ware, and a few sparse pots and pans. Thrilled at the prospect of making a real home at last, I walked through the house, envisioning where I would place each piece of furniture and painting. However, the icing on the cake was that my parents were planning to come and help us unpack.

Having my mom (the one married to my dad) by my side, advising me where to place the "everyday" glasses as opposed to the spot to store the crystal, was the most reassuring feeling a girl could have. As my go-to gal—the one I rang when the kids were sick—the one I called upon with a problem too embarrassing to divulge, even to my therapist—my mom was the person I could say anything to, with absolutely no fear of judgment. She was my biggest fan and sympathizer, and now she would join my dad, coming to aid us, when simply no one else would do.

Life couldn't be better! A visit from my parents, Charles and I would finally transform our home into the masterpiece I had imagined, and then I would begin my most prized creation, other than my kids—something I could be proud of—my book. With a spring in my step, I became elated. Marsha noticed my change in mood and warned me of my limitations. "Your energy level is about two-fold, Shannon. You seem like you may be hypo-manic."

Enjoying the euphoric ride too much to admit to the boundaries I might be crossing, I made a mental note to *act* more controlled. However, that was the problem, for although my body slowed down, a fiesta had already erupted inside me, filling my safe bubble with too much energy, a dangerous plight for someone like me—and we all know what happens when these vesicles expand rapidly—pop!

So my high passed quickly, rolling itself into a train wreck in which my symptoms began to exhibit themselves. Initially, they made a subtle entrance. As people posted statements about being crazy on Facebook, I wondered if they were talking about me.

However, I didn't recognize what was happening until an incident occurred during a short shopping spree. While purchasing an abstract sculpture for my home, the clerk commented on our similar tastes. Her words bounced right out of her mouth and into the air, turning a somersault before landing in my ears as, "You and I are the same. We're both out of our minds."

I knew then that, once again, psychosis had penetrated my skull and taken up residence in my brain, and that soon everyone, including Charles, my children, and close friends, would switch languages; each word would carry multiple meanings, and the world would watch me yet again!

No longer a rookie, I chose to face my relapse head on, gathering indomitable armor and standing my ground in the heat of battle.

Immediately, I called Charles and informed him, promising to begin my medication again. He asked me to notify Marsha, and I said that I would tell her in our next session. Then I returned home and opened up an old friend in my computer tablet: my journal.

Journal
February 3

I abandoned my journal last June. Circumstances have led me back. Since then I went a little crazy, temporarily recovered, returned to the U.S., moved into our new home, and decided to write a book.

Apparently, psychosis slipped into our shipment. How it passed through customs is a wonder. What does this mean? It could be that everything I write is from my own delusions. I can only discern truth in my personal feelings. No other observations are to be trusted until I'm stable again.

Encore

I'm grateful for Charles. He moderates my environment and doesn't allow my temperature to reach dangerous levels. How would I manage without his stability? Thank God for his unconditional love. He's my rock, and I don't want to forget that.

Action plan: *begin medication tonight and inform Dr. Russo Thursday. If she recommends that I spend a few days in the hospital, comply.* **Do not put my family through the same ordeal they suffered last summer.**

That evening I curled up in my lover's lap, laying my head on his shoulder as he relaxed in his favorite chair. "I'm sorry to do this to you again."

He wrapped his arms around me and kissed my cheek. "It's not your fault. It's the illness."

"Why are you so good to me?"

"Because I love you and refuse to let you go."

"Thanks for holding on."

"Thank you for letting me."

I sat up and faced Charles. "I've been thinking about something."

My husband frowned. "Please don't let it be a delusion."

"It's about the kids."

"What?"

"They went through so much last summer. Can we not tell them about this?"

I felt his body stiffen. "We can't keep something like *this* from them, Shannon. Besides, I may need their help. What if you get so that you won't talk to me anymore?"

"I won't. I'm resolved. Plus, I'm doing pretty well now, aren't I?"

"Yes," he admitted, "but we don't know how things will go. Brian warned us that psychosis tends to be worse the second time."

"Can we please just try," I pleaded.

Charles closed his eyes. "We'll try," he agreed.

My heart swelled. This beautiful, beautiful man loved me beyond question.

"I have to tell you something," I confided to Marsha.

Working diligently not to raise her eyebrows, my therapist replied, "And?"

"I'm having symptoms."

"Are you taking your medication? Have you notified your psychiatrist?"

"I started the Latuda last night. My psychiatrist makes me uncomfortable."

"I know someone nearby. Her name is Dr. Sun. She's excellent, and I often refer clients to her. May I give you her number?"

"Yes, please."

Swiftly, but gracefully, she wrote the numbers and letters proposed, and then handed me the paper. "I'll call and explain your circumstances. Perhaps that will expedite things."

Chapter Thirteen:

Optimism

ONCE UPON A time, parents assembled at the city park, desperate for adult companionship and an open space for their bundles of energy to erupt.

Settled in the center of this plaza, a merry-go-round beckoned each little rascal as she piled on, joining the masses until fingers and toes hung off the sides. The edge reserved a spot for a favored few—the most advantageous position—as with one hand clutched to the rail, the other was free to dare wind and gravity to hurl the child from the iron circle that whirled her into euphoria.

But one ill-fated fellow arrived last, restricting himself to spinning those lucky bastards with the sweat of his brow, pull of his arm, and push of his feet. In the world of disorder, we call this chump Lunacy. Begrudging his hard luck, he retaliates. First, he deceives us, leisurely cranking us into a manageable twirl.

Strategically placing myself in the most favorable post on this whirling contraption, I presumed an easy ride—feeling encouraged about my prognosis. *Last time, this demon caught me off-guard, taking possession of my body and mind. He had the advantage and I had not yet acquired the proper tools,* I reassured myself. *But this time, he will not throw me off my feet and into that other world.*

Marsha studied me. "You look thin."

"It's my appetite. I'm trying to enjoy food, but it tastes bland."

"Are you able to eat at all?"

"I'm trying—couldn't finish my cereal this morning."

"Is *anything* good to you?"

"I thought perhaps blueberries would be, so I opened a pack, but they left a bitter taste in my mouth.

Marsha leaned forward. "What are you going to do, Shannon? You have to eat."

"Stick to healthy foods and nuts and hopefully, maintain a weight above one hundred pounds until my mind returns to baseline."

Marsha suggested a plan. "Let's make a deal."

"What?" I asked.

"If your weight goes below one hundred, you admit yourself into the hospital."

Wishing to avoid last summer's episode, I consented. "I will."

No matter what, I was determined to return to sanity: Emerald City, I metaphorically called it. Bound to stay on the right path, I kept a positive outlook and resolved to take my time and do this right. My journal kept me accountable.

Journal
February 4

"Life has options" is my motto. When barriers are placed before me, I naturally become strategic. Once I get over the "Oh shit!" moment, "How can I reach my destination?" automatically pops into my head.

Perhaps I need to step back and examine this reaction. The roadblock could force me to stop in a town I would otherwise have overlooked. Should I enjoy a cup of coffee at the local diner while I review my map? Meanwhile, I might learn about an interesting little museum just behind Main Street. I could stumble upon an old lady who shares colorful stories from days past. A wise person once told me to stop rushing toward the finish line. Life is not a race.

Emerald City is still on my bucket list, but rather than hasten, I will allow myself to penetrate this moment and grow from it.

I did everything in my power to mimic sanity for my children's sake, baking them cookies after school, playing basketball with Jean, chauffeuring them to activities, and helping with homework. However, carrying on a conversation with them frazzled my thoughts and sapped my energy. Their words flew this way and that, garbling into one meaning and then another. In an effort to avoid incomprehensible responses, I kept them as crisp as possible, but it was evident that I was not myself.

Consequently, their behavior altered as well. Jean became more demanding, displaying outbursts of emotion. Don avoided me as much as he politely could, while Michael immersed himself in his video games.

None of them mentioned my sickness, but later the boys confessed that they understood what was going on. Perhaps that's also why Jean acted out more. She simply could not comprehend why Mom was not behaving the way she should.

I continued taking my medication, with no apparent decrease in symptoms. To aggravate matters, side effects took an early toll. I soothed myself with my journal, recognizing that I had not yet allowed enough time to expect results, abiding in my unswerving conviction to stay on my meds.

Journal
February 5

I'm suffering from mild depression induced by the Latuda. Desolation affects me like muscle cramps. It constricts suddenly, then releases almost as quickly as it appeared. Family, friends, and happy thoughts relieve the discomfort.

I will remain steadfast until psychosis surrenders.

Charles paced the room behind me. I closed my laptop and turned around, prepared for a lecture. "You don't like it."

My husband feigned an incredulous look. "Don't like what?"

"You've circled the room the entire time I've been writing. It obviously upsets you."

"It's not that I mind that—just that your behavior's changed."

"I'm being completely open with you this time. The first thing I did when I recognized symptoms was tell you. What can I say? Writing helps. Talking—confuses me."

"But you *need* to talk to *me*, Shannon."

"What am I doing now?"

"You spend more time communicating with your laptop these days."

How could I drive my point home with this man? "You're right, but I have to discuss my problems with someone who *truly* understands what I'm going through, and the only logical person is myself. *No one* else does."

Slumping his shoulders in defeat, Charles nodded. "Okay. I get it, but I still want you to confide in me. I *am* your husband."

"I will." And at that moment, I meant it.

Optimism

I waved the papers in my psychologist's face. "Two pages!"

"Two pages?"

"That's all I wrote before this damn break!"

"Two pages of what, Shannon?"

"Of my book! Of my book!"

"I see. You're frustrated because your psychosis interfered with writing your book."

"Exactly." My heart started to settle.

"You can't focus?"

"Indeed! I promised myself that I wouldn't rush this recovery. I told myself that taking baby steps might be the safest route." My head fell into my hands, which twisted to and fro. "I just didn't count on this. I didn't think I would have writer's block."

Marsha spoke in a soothing tone. "Aren't you keeping a journal?"

I raised my head to see where she was going. "Yes."

"Isn't *this* what your book is about?"

"Yes."

"You know what I think, Shannon?"

"What?"

"I think you've just stumbled upon material for your story. Consider this the research phase of your project."

Man! This lady knew how to make a point.

Now, if I could just make myself eat—

Journal
February 7

As I force-fed myself this morning, it occurred to me that what the sixth sense, psychosis, adds to your sight must be stolen from the tongue. The chore of eating exhausts me. My mouth remains fickle. At times, I enjoy a glimmer of flavor, and then I'm once again raped of that pleasure.

I will not waver on my meds until baseline returns.

West University, Houston's posh shopping and medical district welcomed my pocketbook and me. Today, though, I settled on a gourmet coffee from a corner shop next to my new psychiatrist's building. My watch pointed to ten. *Damn! I'm late.* Running quickly out one door and through the next, I checked in at the desk and found a spot to wait. I sipped my latte, awaiting the woman who would recall my sanity, all the while surveying the room. Refined contemporary paintings and sculptures illuminated the lobby. *She must be good to be able to afford an office here*, I encouraged myself.

Promptly, a petite, but stunning brunette adorned in garments elegantly befitting the room introduced herself to me. "Shannon?"

"Hi, Dr. Sun. It's nice to meet you. Thank you for fitting me in so quickly."

"No problem. Dr. Russo explained your circumstances, and I'm glad to help. Please follow me to my office."

I entered a small opulent office. Her soft, but professional demeanor demanded respect. Sitting on the gray leather miniature couch facing her desk, I waited for her to speak.

"Shannon, please describe your symptoms, giving me a brief background of your condition."

"We relocated to the U.S. from Beijing recently. I suffered a psychotic break that began approximately last May. I was first hospitalized in China and then evacuated to the U.S., where I spent an additional two weeks as an inpatient and one more in outpatient treatment. Mild symptoms returned about a week ago."

The interview continued until Dr. Sun felt well informed.

"Does the Latuda work for you?"

"It makes me depressed."

"Let's try something else."

She scribbled a prescription. "Try this and see me in two weeks. At that point, we should notice results. If you begin to have any adverse effects, please call immediately."

Heeding her advice, I replaced my white pill with a blue one.

Optimism

Reassured, I traded one medication for another, more cutting edge form. My psychiatrist had offered me a new route to my metaphorical destination, and I appreciated her direction.

Journal
February 8

Roadblocks, coffee shops, and retrospect invigorate the mind! I've found a new route to Emerald City. A friendly truck driver pointed it out to me. "Although less traveled, this road hosts extraordinary surprises missed on the freeway," she said.

I prefer unconventional paths anyway. Why not?

That Saturday, I played the soundtrack to *Evita*. Our house was a mess and cleaning it offered me an opportunity to look busy and avoid bewildering dialogue with anyone in my family. However, that was not to be, and it led to my first big confrontation with Charles during this episode.

"Will you please turn down the volume of your CD?"

"I need it to help me focus on my work," I responded.

"I'm trying to work and I don't really like this music," he belted out.

You don't like Evita? "Why not?"

"It's not really my style—a little over the top."

She was not fake! She was a true Matriarch! "I don't agree with you."

Charles stood up from his chair and walked over to me to keep from screaming. "You don't have to agree. Just please lower the volume. It's too loud for me to think."

Now you're calling her loud? "She was not loud, Charles."

He closed his eyes in frustration. "You can't even hear me. I said that the *music* is too loud."

I hear you loud and clear, mister! "I'll turn it down, but take back what you said about Evita."

"I'm talking about the fucking CD, Shannon."

You just called her a slut! I can't believe you called her a slut! I lowered my voice, so as to make the seriousness of my message clear. "Evita Peron may not have been perfect. But she did what she could for her country the best way she knew how."

Befuddlement poured over my husband's face. "Please just turn the volume down."

I complied, stomping out of the room to abandon my chores and make my way toward my own laptop.

Journal
February 9

As Charles and I listened to the soundtrack to Evita just now, the colossal thorn of our marriage dug deeply into my side. He belittled Evita Peron, a woman I consider a Matriarch and heroine to the Argentinian people, calling her a slut!

This moment personifies an attitude about women that I believe reflects masculine issues. Don't get me wrong. I love men. They're 50% of what is good about the human race. What pisses me off is when one member of a group underestimates others.

I feel devalued as a representative of the feminine gender! My small stature and southern charm might lead others to believe I'm fragile. They are sorely mistaken. I AM WOMAN! HEAR ME ROAR!!

Chapter Fourteen:

Remorse

MY THERAPIST ENCOUNTERED psychosis many times in the hospitals she frequented early on in her career. She understood the correlation between my connected dots and disconnected relationships and did everything in her power to cement mine with Charles into an unbreakable form.

"In your last episode, Charles was your enemy, right?"

"Sort of. I certainly thought he was out to get me—and I guarded myself from him. But I also felt compelled to protect him."

"Why?"

"Who would otherwise?"

"And this time?"

"I'm fighting it."

"How?"

"When I was sick before, I kept a force-field around myself."

"You didn't let him in."

"Right. But he refused to leave, venturing as close as I'd allow."

"What did he do? How did he handle it?"

"He came to the hospital every day, letters, poems, and cards in hand. Before that, he brought me flowers."

"Did it help?"

"Not at the time. I thought it was all an act."

"That must've hurt him."

"He told me afterwards that it was the most painful experience of his life. I keep two cards in my wallet to remind me. Would you like to see?"

"Why don't you read them, Shannon?"

"Sure."

Opening the first, I relayed his message.

My Darling Shannon,

My love for you will never die nor stop, no matter how hard you push away. I took a vow over nineteen years ago to protect you, to love you, to care for you. My vow stands!

I love you,
Charles

Marsha waited. She wanted the words I read to sink in. "That sounds quite convincing."

"Would you like to hear the other?"

"Of course!"

My Dearest Shannon,

Each day that I think of you, that I see you, that I hear you, I see beauty that only these roses can begin to imitate. My lady, my teacher, my mother, my best friend, my love, my life, my WIFE.

I LOVE YOU!!
Charles

Remorse

Folding her hands in her lap, my therapist leaned in and looked me square in the eyes. "Those sound like the words of a soul mate, Shannon."

Shaking my head to ensure it was in the game, I acceded. "I *must remember* this time that he's sincere."

Glancing at the cards in confirmation, she concurred. "Well—there's your proof."

Clinging to my promise not to "forget" this time, I dug my feet into the ground by the door that shut out my husband.

Journal
February 10

As I contemplate the divides between Charles and me, it's important to consider our personality differences. He's an apple and I'm an orange. No matter how hard I squeeze, Charles can't produce nectar he doesn't have. In return, I don't make a palatable apple pie. However, he's a good apple–and I can be quite refreshing.

Friends and family endeavored earnestly to soothe my malaise. Rebecca and Ollie dropped by with strawberries and cards. Then Ling called and insisted on catching the next plane from Beijing to Houston. My mom also implored me to let her come and stay with us for awhile. However, I asked Rebecca and Ollie to give me space and declined my mom's and Ling's offers. As much as I loved and appreciated them all, the thought of any social exchange outside of Charles and the kids overwhelmed me.

Aware of their heartfelt intentions, I sent a group email to my closest friends and requested their patience, as my texts, calls, and visits would probably be sparse until I was my old self again. Because I have excellent taste in people, they each replied with genuinely sympathetic words, allowing me as much breathing room as I needed.

Around that time, two more symptoms began to haunt me. Dr. Russo checked them out thoroughly, peeking under each rock in the path.

"Are you having hallucinations?"

"Words—flashbacks."

"Do you hear Valentino?"

"Not Valentino—other voices."

"I've never experienced psychosis, Shannon. Educate me."

I searched the wall's corners for a plausible description. "Science states this condition affects the neurotransmitters in my brain and ignites a chemical change, but that doesn't explain the physical transformation."

"What physical transformation?"

"My skull."

"What about your skull?"

Knocking my fist against my head, I explained. "This hard shell protecting my mainframe mutates into marmalade."

"Are you saying it becomes jammed?"

"It invites penetration."

Marsha knew not to laugh. "So you're getting screwed."

"Constantly, by unsolicited visions and language."

"How do you protect yourself?"

"I think I should invest in a hard hat."

Finally, Charles approached me with his concerns about my behavior around the children. Michael and Don had both informed him that they had found me sitting in the same chair and position each day after school for a week now. Home-cooked meals were also becoming more and more basic.

"If you don't want the kids to know about your illness," he advised, "you need to do a few things around the house."

My communication skills had distorted to such a degree that I couldn't explain properly why I had limited my movement. The truth was that any activity exacerbated my symptoms, as if the motion of my body prompted activity in my brain.

However, my husband was right about the kids. If I truly wanted to protect them, I had to do my part at least to feign lucidity. Thus, I took them to a family fun palace as an outing after school. At first, my symptoms faded behind the wheel of my go-kart. Chasing one another around a tire-encased asphalt track released me momentarily from psychotic interruptions, allowing me to enjoy the kids' company freely and completely. However, when I stepped out of the buggy and into the gallery, circumstances changed. Flashing arcade lights and a host of patrons' voices invaded my senses, sending my mind into overdrive. I allowed Michael, Don, and Jean to have their fill of the games, but all the while, I paced the floor with a paranoid eye, wishing desperately to escort them home safely, as I was certain that some pedophile was lurking, biding his time to seize my babies, and drag them to his hideout.

Language was not all that became muddled. Apparently, so did time.

Journal
March 11

Finally, I noticed my blunder. Apparently, psychosis affected my inner clock.☺ I've been marking recent dates as February, when, in fact, it's March.

Twisting My Kaleidoscope

Marsha probed. "So, you still aren't hearing Valentino, the voice you fell in love with last year?"

"No, they're random this time. I try to keep my distance from that one."

"Valentino?"

"Yes."

"Why him?"

"I don't want to go there again."

"What will you do if he shows up at the door?"

"I doubt I'll invite him in."

"How will you do that, if you can't keep the others out?"

"He's different."

"How?"

"He wouldn't push himself on me. He only wants to help."

"You don't want the help?"

"That's not what I'm afraid of."

"What frightens you, then?"

"The relationship."

"But he's not real, Shannon. You know that."

I sighed. "I understand. But the feelings he transmits are authentic."

"So, you're telling me that this fictional character has some sort of power over you, even though you're sure he's a figment of your imagination."

"Exactly."

Chapter Fifteen:

DO YOU REMEMBER how that sullen and vengeful Lunacy—the one who was relegated to pushing the merry-go-round in my scenario—began to express his outrage with deception? Respect his fraudulent artistry. For just as I *thought* I had the upper hand, he darted into a ferocious sprint, accelerating the "joyride" into a full-blown cyclone. Dangling over the rim, I presumed my weight could overpower his tenacity, but he proved to be a worthy adversary with an army to boot.

Desolation assaulted me, mocking my tenacity, as I questioned every word and motive, no matter the source. This unwelcome ailment had pulled me from my safe position and set me down in the center of a war zone. Immediately, a delusion shot from the west, then a hallucination from the east. Progressing swiftly, symptoms came at me from every direction at such speeds I could barely dance rapidly enough to dodge injury. Consequently, I also began to doubt my reality. Was I crazy? Were these truly delusions? *Or* had the world deceived me? I was no longer sure.

Journal
March 14

 If I'm an orange, I feel that I've been peeled, squeezed, chewed, and spit into the trash. My illness has become malignant, spreading from my head to my heart. Somehow, this hole in my middle organ increased its density to a nearly unbearable weight.

 Which is worse: being delusional and recognizing it, or the fear loitering at the edge of my mind that it is in fact a reality? I doubled my medication today, with approval from my psychiatrist. My lack of discernment tortures me.

 I fear that I'm being watched by the world again. Images of dancing in my bathroom naked, intimate conversations, provocative moments with my husband, taunt me. Have they been on display for others' entertainment? My privacy has been violated!

 The knife digs deeper if I consider all of those who are "dear to me," who must know, and who would allow me to humiliate myself and my family publicly. WHO WOULD EVER CHOOSE THIS? I CERTAINLY HAVEN'T. If so, does anyone actually care enough to make it stop?

 I'm broken-hearted that my husband would promote such a farce–that a man I gave my ultimate trust and love to would be a part of such a cruel endeavor.

 Oh, please take these thoughts out of my head. They puncture my pores and bleed me dry.

    Sleep eluded me that evening. I simply could not close my eyes until I determined whether or not I was inundated by delusions or schemers. Immersed in rumination for eight long hours, I reviewed scenes of my life, creating a pattern of connected dots from one event to the next. When the sun rose, I came to a conclusion.

Certain now that the world did indeed hold me under both a microscope and microphone, it was "clear" that every thought I had, whether it be by cognition, mouth, or hand, was exposed to the world, and because I could hide nothing, I addressed my planet directly through my journal. You could say it became my blog.

Journal
March 15

Screw it! I'll not edit my thoughts because of some perceived idea of being heard. I wish no harm to anyone and I AM A GOOD PERSON. I WILL allow my cognitive freedom.

If for some bizarre reason, others enter my head and are offended by what they see—STAY THE FUCK OUT!!!!!

I approached my psychologist as "Dr. Marsha Russo" one last time, for this peculiar disease would soon infect our relationship, sending it into an otherworldly realm and changing the way I addressed her.

"You're quiet today, Shannon."

I stared at the face in front of me and saw the same brown eyes and gentle smile. Her soft, husky voice sounded like the confidant I had grown to adore, but could I trust her? "I'm afraid."

"Of what?"

I searched the room for ears. *What a nightmare!* "I don't want to hurt anyone."

"Do the voices want you to do something that might harm someone?"

I shook my head. "No. It's not like that." *Why are you putting words in my mouth?*

"I'm afraid that whatever I say will come back to haunt me—or even worse—deprecate people I care about."

"I'm the only other person in this room, Shannon, and I would lose my license if I shared your information with anyone else."

What good does that do me if you can all read my mind? "It's the delusions."

"Tell me about them."

Better yet, I'll offer you an example. "My parents called last night. They told me about their fishing trip."

"Go on."

"They stated that it's more fun when you actually catch something."

"How does this relate to your delusions?"

"I think they were sending me a message. They were trying to tell me that I was being baited. Every time I say something negative to you about my loved ones, it hooks them."

"How?"

"The entire planet hears."

Realization shone in Marsha's eyes. "And this makes you afraid to share your problems with me."

"I'm only attempting to make sense of my world. If I request your help reconfiguring, it doesn't mean that I wish to sabotage the people in it."

My therapist scrutinized me for several seconds, and then scrawled on her pad before making her next statement. "Shannon, I'm concerned that your medicine may not be working. You seem…" She paused, "drugged today."

Dismay

My psychologist was right. Deception had swirled such a storm inside my head, I felt inebriated by confusion. Alas, I was not a happy drunk.

Every song on the radio sent a message. I attached my ear to the source desperately, dissecting and decoding. Social networks became the paparazzi, scandalizing every move I made.

Determined to confirm my theory, I turned the camera of my laptop toward me in the kitchen and tossed blackberries in the air, catching them in my mouth. Later that evening, I described my plan to Charles, deliberating on his reaction as well as that of society.

He glanced at the time on the oven. "It's nine o'clock. You need to get some sleep. I don't want to take you back to the hospital."

Confident that he heard my thoughts, I smiled, dispatching my meaning telepathically. *Of course you do!* "Heading that way."

"What were you doing in the kitchen—with the blackberries?" My husband's eyes questioned.

So, we're going to "pretend"—I'll entertain your charade. "A little experiment."

"With blackberries?"

"Just to confirm—"

"Confirm what, Shannon? I don't understand."

"I'm going to check Facebook tomorrow—see if anyone posts any jokes about blackberry tossing. I looked silly enough to warrant a joke or two."

Charles looked stricken, as if last summer's nausea had returned to his poor soul's gut.

"Ohhhh—um—okay. I think you need to get some rest."

"Good night. I love you."

"Good night, baby doll—I love you too."

Go ahead. Report this. I KNOW your plan. First, though, I made a quick detour to my laptop as my husband returned cautiously to his own desk.

Journal
March 16

I tested my delusion today–will have to check Facebook to review results. I prefer not to, but it's the only way. Wish me luck. I'm about to jump–

The next day I checked Facebook. Although no blackberry remarks popped out of the screen, I assumed that my husband had tipped everyone off, proving that he was indeed in on the conspiracy. I no longer knew whose intentions I could and could not trust. It left me feeling destitute.

I did, however, consider Marsha my ally and helper, but no longer as my psychologist. She had morphed into the Role Master. Twice a week, I crossed the threshold of a cryptic stage, disguised as her private office. Incapable of determining a pattern assigned to the characters she played—whether one soul or a conglomeration confronted me—I could never predict my company.

Each exchange exposed glimpses of Marsha, reassuring me that she would pop up to assist or mediate when necessary. Most often, however, I conversed with the other voices that consumed her. In my eyes, these were *real* spirits entering her body.

Two months prior, I had expressed a need to face my demons head on. She granted my wish as I confronted each soul that occupied her.

At this point, her words no longer formed linear sentences. Grammar rearranged itself mystically to disclose the unfeigned meaning buried beneath the literal. My efforts to disentangle each message and respond appropriately slowed my response time.

Dismay

I often countered with my mind what my lips refused to disclose. Convinced that she listened on both accounts, I returned home each day resolved that the hour had concluded with mutual understanding.

Today, she would be the radio DJ.

"Do you still feel like the world is watching you?" she asked.

Of course! Because it is! "Yes."

"And hearing your thoughts?"

Allow me to clarify as I scream from this platform you placed me on! "Have you ever read *A Wrinkle in Time*?"

"No, I can't say I have."

"It's my favorite childhood book."

"Tell me about it."

"The main characters travel to a planet in another galaxy to face 'IT'."

"An evil alien?"

"A giant brain."

"But evil nevertheless."

"Yes. As vassals of IT, every inhabitant in that world relinquishes free will."

"So, they're all controlled by one mind."

"Yep."

"And you feel a bit like IT."

"Yes, with two critical exceptions."

"What are those, Shannon?"

"I'm not evil and I have no desire to play motherboard."

Convinced that some anomic deviation of nature had delivered me into this world with metaphysical potential, I wondered why such information had been withheld from me. "Who am I?" and "Why would they do this?" preoccupied me.

An obsessive curiosity overcame me. God must have made me this way for a reason. I *needed* to understand why.

Twisting My Kaleidoscope

Journal
March 17

This mysterious mind provokes me one way or another. I close my eyes. Psychosis forces them open. It straps the kaleidoscope to my head and twists me in all angles against my will. I have no choice but to look at each pattern. When blurry, I'm mocked. After focusing the lens, reality smites me. Am I angry? Yes! Am I hurt? Yes! Am I confused? Yes! Wouldn't you be?

I stopped taking my medication.

Chapter Sixteen:

Destiny?

DETESTING THE THOUGHT of the world making a game out of my circumstances, I commissioned literature as a tutor, in the hope that it would at least shed some light on my situation, reading every book I could get my hands on. I was sure they each held a clue to my perplexing condition, and I was certain that the more I read, the closer I would come to solving the answers of my riddled life.

Journal
March 18

I'm coming to terms with my situation. Thanks to Maya Angelou and Kahlil Gibran, a piece of peace now settles in my little finger. Perhaps it will envelop my whole hand tomorrow. I must be patient.

My book—I want to write. Is that what I am doing now?

Shall I call it "Chaotic Elegance"?

Each time I entered church, hyper-religiosity and grandiosity threatened to possess me, pressuring me to become their Jesus, a role I did not wish to play. This overpowering presence took every bit of strength I had to ward off.

"Open your Bibles to Luke fifteen, verses eleven through thirty-two," our minister announced, innocently setting off alarms in my head.

Why do you have to go there?

"Because today we're going to review God's Love for us," he continued.

Under normal circumstances, my surname admits advantages, but imagine the implications of this title for a delusional individual. Can you see how, in such a state of mind, one might confuse the word "love" as a form of personal address? For me, that's what happened. I believed sincerely that each time this very common word was used, that the speaker was indicating it (love) to be me. On this particular day, I assumed the preacher had announced that God sent *me*, His *Love*, to earth.

I'm not who you think I am, I tried to inform our pastor.

He then rolled out Jesus' parable, The Prodigal Son, expounding on how the father's unconditional adoration for his squandering child mirrored our Savior's love for us. Thereafter, he moved into his last statement. "When God sent us his son, he sent his *Love*."

However, I offered the final words, transposing my thoughts through the air. *I really am not who you think I am.*

I left church ill at ease. Forcing the world to follow me, an imperfect being, in mindless obedience, lurched far from my moral principles. Ethically, I could not accept such a portrayal.

Charles drove home, allowing me time to ruminate. I thought of horrific leaders from the past, such as Hitler and Mussolini, who

Destiny?

spawned calamity from a marriage of their demented ideas with blind loyalty on the part of their followers. Although I did not consider myself destructive, I did have trouble discerning fantasy from truth. My reality was muddled. I was still lucid enough to comprehend that.

Think for yourselves! I wanted to scream. I addressed the matter subtly in my "blog."

Journal
March 19

Do we really need to FOLLOW a leader like sheep? Can we not view our circumstance and THINK?

"Will this hurt anyone?"

"Do I have good intentions?"

"What will be the consequences of my actions?"

I blunder continuously, but will not cease to use this organ beneath my skull. It's my RESPONSIBILITY to recognize the miscalculation and the only TRUE way to learn and grow.

Otherwise, history repeats itself. Some parts are worth recurring; others could use a bit of tweaking. I'm a work in progress and am okay with that.

Like my first break, mood swings—predominantly in the form of mania—set the pace and direction of my illness. A cocktail of delusions, hallucinations, and irrational thoughts raced through my brain, rapidly spinning me into exhaustion. To make matters worse, my collapsing appetite left me with sunken eyes and baggy jeans. My outside self now bore evidence of my disheveled insides.

This atrocity burned through my husband's eyes. I could see it choking him, as he tried to reach the woman he married. However, I didn't trust him and believed him to be disingenuous. After twenty years of marriage, my soul mate could detect insincerity in how I responded to him.

"You're growing apart from me again," he droned.

"I'm tired."

Charles wrapped his arms around my waist. Every part of me stiffened. He ignored it and voiced his concerns. "I know. You aren't sleeping; I feel you tossing and turning all night."

Like you care! You're probably pleased at this mess I'm in. "I'll try to be more still."

He stroked my hair. I didn't like it.

"I'm just worried about you, that's all." He pulled back momentarily to scan the garments that draped my body shapelessly. "Are you still over one hundred pounds?"

Ha! I eat three meals a day, mister. No chance of you dragging me back to that place again. "The scale said one hundred three this morning. I'm hanging in there—don't need to go to the hospital yet."

Charles looked stricken. He could read my body better than anyone could. He could sense my remoteness. He squeezed me tighter, as if to hold on to the "ghost" I claimed to be to him a year ago. For, in spirit, that's what I had become.

"I love you, Shannon! *Please* don't leave me," he pleaded.

"I'm not going anywhere," I replied. *I wouldn't give you that satisfaction. If you want to escape, then* you *will be the one taking off, not me.*

"Me neither, baby. You're my angel, and we'll get through this somehow."

I raised my face up to this stranger, searching his eyes. *Do I even really know you?*

Destiny?

My husband held me awhile longer, perhaps waiting for some sort of reciprocation of his affections. I allowed the moment without challenge, but my hostility barricaded any warmth between us.

As I refused to play the roles society attempted to force upon me, I felt sure they chose to turn me into a fool, as a punishment—throwing invisible pie in my face each time I stepped into public. Finding my spot on Marsha's stage, I wondered who she would be and if the specter within her could help impress upon my planet the unhealthy demands it made on me. As good fortune would have it, allies of my resistance possessed her this time.

"Are you getting out of the house, Shannon?"

"I force myself."

"What challenges you most?"

You sent my friends today. "Conversation with anyone saps me. I reserve that energy for my family."

"Can you attend to tasks such as grocery shopping, and taking your children to activities and doctor's appointments?"

Focusing on the twiddling thumbs in my lap, I paused. "Yes."

"You hesitated."

"Do you remember our 'word penetration' discussion?"

"I recall you mentioning an attack of verbal invasion."

"Larger crowds launch more bullets."

"So they paralyze you."

"I'm too headstrong for that. But they create an unpleasant experience."

"What upsets you the most?"

Thank you for asking! Let's establish a few ethics for these folks. "Church and shopping."

"Why church?"

Tell them to stop trying to make me Jesus! "They ram their thumbs against my temples!"

"The ones beside your eyes?" my psychologist chuckled.

I couldn't help but grin back. "Yeah."

"That's a lot of pressure."

"They're hell bent on forcing my compliance."

This time laughter bellowed out of her. "An interesting way to put it."

You know it's true. "It's not a fair fight—all of them against one of me."

"Why do you go?"

"It's nice to have an avenue—to commemorate my spirituality."

"Is it worth it?"

"Not if it becomes a hassle."

"And what about the shopping? That isn't fun anymore?"

"The feeling of being watched by the world spawns suspicions of being a walking commercial."

"You resent that."

It's wrong. "It makes me uncomfortable."

Why was this happening? I simply could not fathom why such an occurrence would come in the middle of my life. A conversation with my second son helped me sort it out.

"Mom, did you know that Stan Lee didn't become a success until he was about your age?" Don informed me one afternoon.

"Huh? Who's that?"

"He's the creator of Marvel comics—you know—Spider Man—X-men."

Did he have powers like me? "How did he accomplish it?"

"He just came up with an amazing idea and captured an audience."

Destiny?

Is that why I'm going through this? Is my book the purpose?

At this point, no longer convinced that I was psychotic, I couldn't actually comprehend what my book was about anymore. I just felt compelled to write it. My predicament became a pile of lemons, meant to be squeezed and mixed with just the right ingredients to concoct the perfect recipe for my memoir, and that meant that I must first do my research and figure out what was real and what was not.

Journal
March 19

How did I get here? Will I ultimately understand my situation? May I color code truth and deception?

Reflection! Reflection! Reflection! I must look backwards and forwards and rearrange this furniture within me. If I nick my shin on the table in the dark, it ought to be moved. Then reasonably, I can beg my pardon and attend to the lemons, my kitchen counter supports.

What about those lemons, Shannon? Companionless, they wrench my face, contort my lips, and shrink my tongue. But, with a bit of water and sugar, the muscle my mouth abodes lavishes, subsequently protruding out to lick what might have escaped. Yes, I will partake of this yellow fruit and utilize the nutrients inside.

Chapter Seventeen:

Rodeos

WRITING IN METAPHOR safeguarded those entwined in my delusions, while granting perusal of each complexity. It was my way of addressing sensitive issues without encroaching upon my privacy or that of others. Nevertheless, sometimes I really did go to the rodeo.

Journal
March 22

Yesterday we took the train to the rodeo. Apparently, so did the rest of Houston, for a large crowd packed itself tightly into the same caravan—escalating my social anxiety almost to panic. Recognizing my discomfort, Charles and the kids surrounded me. I prayed for calm.

Once we entered the arena, the mass of people multiplied into such enormity, I became overwhelmed. My primal brain took over, shifting into survival mode. I simply focused on breathing. Squeezing my legs around the belly of the moment and holding tight to the reins of mere existence exhausted me. But, as they say, the show must go on.

The national anthem and a wagon race inaugurated the chain of competitions. Soon, cowgirls held tight to their horses, swinging them from side to side as they sprinted between barrels, while cowboys risked their lives clinging to agitated beasts attempting to hurtle them to the ground. Wranglers teamed up to rope calves, stronger and heavier than most men—an impressive sight for even the most dispassionate of citizens. And, although the crowd around me clenched teeth with one eye open, my lids drooped and my mouth could not keep from yawning.

Then—the concert began as The Band Perry stepped onstage in the middle of the arena, bringing me to attention. Something about their performance exhilarated and enraptured me. I suppose it could have been the laser-lights that bedazzled my eyes—but there was the music, that ravishing music! I let go, absorbing the sound and lyrics, spellbound.

The melodic stories took me to a different plane, where I experienced another world of words and emotions. The potion veiled my past and future and placed me in its paintings. Flavors, fragrances, textures, and sounds twirled into a waltz that moved my feet until the allure relinquished them.

Was such a concoction healthy? Like magic, it depends on the chemist's intentions. My nature wished to trust. My condition tested this tendency.

All in all, I rode bareback, rested up for the next round, then danced with the bull.

Incapable of enjoying socialization of any sort, I accepted a dinner invitation with two close lesbian friends the following day. Consequently, the perplexing language I spoke infested our conversation, creating an absurd scene in my head.

As my girlfriend apologized for preparing stuffed chicken, when she had promised us beef stroganoff, I tossed her words in the air, concocting my own interpretation. It came out something like this: "I thought you were our champion, you big *chicken*! Why didn't you announce your homosexuality to the world as you were supposed to? You let me down. You let us all down. You should be ashamed of yourself, abandoning the gay community like that!"

That's not fair! I can't help it that I'm attracted to men, I retorted telepathically. Conflicted by a combination of guilt and frustration, I made my closing remark. *Why would you demand such a thing from me? You, of all people, should empathize with how it would feel to be forced to pretend one sexual orientation when, in fact, you are another!*

Of course my friends couldn't fathom what was going through my mind that evening, but it ended in hugs and exhaustion for all of us. For psychotic tension can be sensed, even by the sane.

Journal
March 23

I'm an open book and my print blazes in bright, bold red and every other color and anxiety shifts my brain into warp speed–not good for me or the company I'm with.

But a genuine friend not only appreciates my agreeable parts, but also respects the bits that flow upstream for her. And if I love her with the same authenticity, I too will regard her attitudes and wishes with deference.

I left my laptop so fatigued, pajamas took effort—and teeth—well, they would go un-brushed.

"*Identify yourself!*" echoed around me. "*Your ambiguity annoys us.*" Why did the world mandate such decisiveness? Its demands seemed unfair. I wished someone—anyone—would come to my aid. That's when Jean stepped loyally to my side and asked me to play the *Would You Rather* game. I accepted wholeheartedly, praying it would serve my purpose as an opportunity to denounce the imposed labels I thought humanity wished to place on me, both verbally and clairvoyantly.

"Mom, would you rather have a puppy or a kitten?"

"I fancy both the playfulness of a puppy *and* the comfort of a kitten."

"Mom! You're supposed to choose one or the other."

"Keep going. Ask me another one."

"Which would be more fun, a son or a daughter?"

"I could never choose. They're both a blast."

"You stink at this game."

"Try again."

"Which color do you prefer, red, or blue?"

"It depends on my mood."

"Mom!" Jean pouted. "I don't want to play anymore."

"Try one more," I suggested.

"Okay, would you rather have an elephant or a lion as a pet?"

"Neither. They aren't meant to be kept in captivity."

My daughter stamped her foot and shrieked, "I'm trying to have a little fun with you and you have to get all 'serious' with me! Why can't you just make a choice?"

Genuinely believing that I was addressing my entire planet, rather than an eleven-year-old girl, I justified my remarks calmly.

Rodeos

"You're asking too much from me. I don't yet have definitive answers."

The annoyance in her eyes left, making room for bewilderment. She then voiced a valid statement. "You can be so weird sometimes."

I tousled her hair and responded, "Thanks, kiddo." *Thanks for helping me put some sense back into this crazy world.*

Journal
March 25

Why does it make people so uncomfortable when I choose not to label myself. Can't I just BE? Is it necessary for me to add absolute titles? May I please just be ME?

Chapter Eighteen:

My Tablet

CONVINCED THAT MUSIC sent direct messages to me, I felt mistreated by its unkind lyrics, so I allowed my therapist's stage to be my platform for a plea. *Please stop mocking me!* I screamed telepathically.

Greeting me as the personage of Dr. Rostami, Marsha voiced her observation. "You've lost it."

I don't want it. It's not healthy—for anyone. "Lost what?"

"Your smile. It's gone."

"I can't listen to music anymore." *They ruined it for me.*

"The messages?"

They mock me. "They're—troublesome."

Marsha searched her notes for help. "What kind of music do you like?"

"All kinds."

"Your favorite?"

"I guess country."

"Do you prefer male or female singers?"

"I like both."

"Why?"

"Because it would be boring otherwise."

"I'm going to send you a download of a new song, written by two young artists. Focus on their words."

That evening I listened as they sang to their sweet melody.

"*Don't fret. It is already written.*"

Emphasizing the bottom line, they sang their message clearly. Worrying wastes energy. Perhaps my plans had already been made. Possibly, I wrote them myself and had the power to fight these delusions by merely typing my true wishes in my tablet. Soon after, my weary head rested soundly for the first time in weeks, allowing refreshment of my spirit and imparting perspective the next morning.

Had I not stopped taking my medication after all? I was sure no pills had slid down my throat for awhile now. However, there was something else that helped, something my pharmacist did not deliver. I walked to my desk and scrutinized the laptop upon it. Eagerly opening it to the journal inside, I realized the tablet I digested daily confirmed the singers' wisdom. "*No worries, Shannon. Here it is—already written.*"

What did this mean? My journal was my *true* medication.

Journal
March 25

I feel empowered and now understand how to master my condition. Efficacy is the most magnificent medicine!

It turns out that the words on my tablet required many doses for complete digestion. Angst regarding my circumstances menaced every essence of my being for days to come. Dreams imposed on me as well as music. Some nights they placated; during others, they coerced. I prayed for repose. Whether they sent positive messages or negative, I associated my dreams with the intentions of the spirits entering my body that evening.

My Tablet

Journal
March 26

My mind plays tricks on me, but my heart remains steady. I'm beginning to understand its strange rhythm. Sometimes it must dance around the chicaneries.

One such incident happened one day when Charles and I were out. While exiting a shop, I held the door for him.

"Thank you, baby doll," my husband responded graciously, an affectionate title he had used to address me for twenty years now.

Ordinarily, I would have returned his sentiment with something like, "You're quite welcome, my love."

Instead, deception played tricks on my mind, projecting Charles into the forefront as a master opponent in this ridiculous competition in which I imagined myself to be. For at that point, I was positive that the world had made a game out of my life—some cruel form of entertainment for everyone's viewing pleasure. I begrudged both my husband and humanity for placing me in the center of it. Moreover, I did not accept his remark as good will. Instead, "You weak little baby! One score against you!" jabbed my twisted ears.

"Don't ever call me that again!" I hissed.

Whack! My words smacked him across the face and his eyes revealed the damage my mouth discharged. "I'm—I'm—sorry." Charles stammered. "I didn't mean it as an insult."

Yes, you did! "That's okay," I replied more calmly. "Just please don't call me that anymore. It's belittling."

That evening I sent a strong message of assertiveness in my tablet. If my planet would not release me from this curse, then I would at least determine the rules.

Journal
March 27

A little guideline in MY game of life: Politeness does not equal weakness, it equates with sophistication and deserves respect!

One day Marsha received me as the specter of my dear friend Dabir, and for a few brief moments, she released the air that constricted me.

"The word artillery, Shannon."

"What about it?"

"Is there any rhyme or reason to it? Does it carry a theme?"

"Many."

"Give me examples."

Dabir! How are you? "You know about colors and numbers—and the game."

"How could I forget? Is this still a game to you?"

It's only a game to THEM—not me. "No."

"Any other themes?" Marsha continued.

"Nicknames."

"Nicknames?"

"Yeah. In the beginning, I was the 'bitch'."

"And how did you translate this?"

"Every time I heard a commercial or read a statement about dogs, it felt like a taunt."

"Did it hurt your feelings?"

"It certainly didn't amuse me."

"How did you respond?"

My Tablet

"I ignored it as much as possible."
"Do any unfashionable labels bug you now?"
"The 'Whine'—spelled W*I*N*E."
"The Wine?"
"I assume it's because people don't appreciate my dissatisfaction with my circumstances."
"Any others?"
"Yeah—'The Cheese'."
"Why?"
"Apparently my 'good attitude' days are considered cheesy."
"Damned if you do, damned if you don't."
"Nah."
"Why not?"
"Because sticks and stones may break my bones, but words will never hurt me."
"Do you believe this?"
"Perhaps if I say it enough, I will."

The taunting hallucinations and delusions took time to puncture me, but enough poking eventually opened wounds. My spirit began to wear thin.

A month had passed since my world turned upside down and I grasped desperately for any thread of hope to hang onto. My life felt like a nightmare, but I simply could not allow myself to envision it that way. I had to believe that there was a purpose for all this. Otherwise, I would give up.

So, I held fast to my Emerald City fantasy. This destination and my book became both my goals and my coping mechanisms. Although my confused state had morphed them into fabrications, like the other delusions, they offered me a positive focus, a light to walk toward in the midst of my otherwise chaotic existence.

Journal
March 29

Would I have taken this path to Emerald City if the truck driver had mentioned the road construction on the way? She was too wise to inform me. Otherwise, I might have chosen another route.

When my nerves fret, the radio finds a tune to soothe them. This trip has discharged every emotion my soul contrives. I've felt more since I left that café than I have in the twenty years prior.

This orange has been squeezed hard. Is any juice left? Emerald City still awaits.

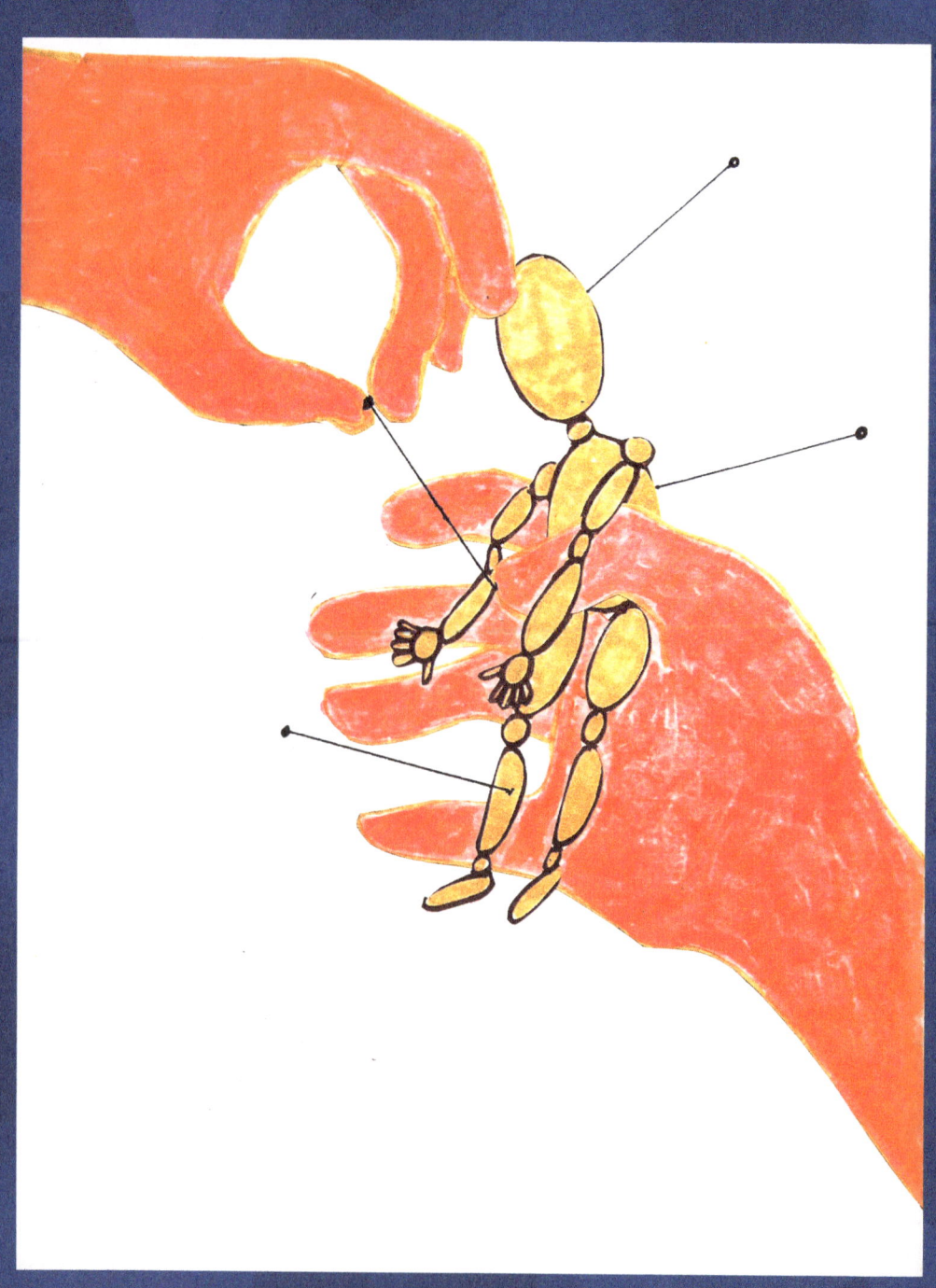

Chapter Nineteen:

Sorcery

JUST LIKE MY first break, my delusions in this episode propagated, one apparition bursting from another. Thus, an incident occurred that led me to believe that my powers were not merely psychical, but could also inflict tangible and irrevocable harm.

It materialized when I was hanging family photos on the wall. I paused to text my sister-in-law, requesting a recent picture of her kids. She responded quickly, asking "Why?" Soon after, her family photo fell to the floor. I considered this a sign that something horrific would happen to them. Perhaps my actions simulated voodoo. Was I actually "hanging" the individual by nailing him to the wall? The sharp whistle of alarm blared, "*Heed your powers! You do not know what they can do.*" It inflamed my apprehensions—I had no idea how to control them. It unnerved me. I didn't want to hurt anyone.

Then suddenly it occurred to me, perhaps I already had. Fear soaked my body with the kind of sweat that burns, just before you freeze.

Journal
April 4

> *I emit a bewitching hex. It casts a spell of smoke—a sorcery I am still unsure of. What damage can it do? What catastrophes have already come from it?*
> *Please be careful, Shannon. Be very careful!*

However, this appalling delusion did not stop there. That night, a dream woke me up, convincing me that Don's previous school had manipulated him into painting a picture of an explosion as a means to eradicate humanity and start over (genocide). I took my son's artwork off my wall and into the garage, where I covered it completely with spray paint.

Furious at the atrocity they had attempted, I screamed telepathically that they had better apologize, make this right, and accept responsibility, or it would be unforgivable. The next morning my daughter played the school's theme song and I forgave them.

Stunned by my actions, Charles phoned Marsha for an emergency session. She and my husband wore the same expression, and I was sure she was there in the guise of my parents. "Talk to me, Shannon."

This isn't fair. You're ganging up on me. "I'm fine. Charles overreacted."

She exchanged glances with the man I accused. "We're both concerned for you, Shannon. Otherwise, I would be puttering in my garden right now, enjoying the afternoon with my husband."

"I'm sorry to take your Saturday, Marsha," Charles said, clearly distressed.

"That's quite all right. I'm glad you called. We just need to emphasize the peculiarity of her behavior—and why it troubles us."

I was furious. *How could you involve my parents, Charles? You went too far!*

Sorcery

"What's so strange? Has neither of you ever suffered a sleepless night?"

Exasperated, my husband rolled his eyes. "That isn't why I called. You know that, Shannon!"

Attempting to defuse the atmosphere, Marsha addressed Charles, "Please relate what happened." Then she looked at me. "Shannon, I want you to *listen*. Try to envision how this might look—to us."

You know why I did it! You should thank me! "I'm all ears," I said.

Charles began. "We watched a movie last night, as a family. It was science fiction, with some violence, and I was proud of Shannon for participating. She struggles with that sort of thing."

Thank God I did!

"Did the brutality bother you, Shannon?" Marsha inquired.

"The main character, a boy about Don's age, was quite gifted."

"Was he killed?"

"Much worse."

"What could be worse?"

"The adults in charge tricked him in an abhorrent way."

"What did they do?"

"They deceived him into committing genocide, using the ruse that it was a 'game'."

"It was only a movie, Shannon," Charles intervened.

Yes—but this is not. "I didn't say it wasn't. Marsha asked me a question and I answered it."

"That's a good point, Shannon," my therapist said in an appeasing tone. "However, Charles and I suspect that it might have led to your actions afterwards."

Of course it did! "I suppose it could be what kept me up."

Marsha moved forward. "Charles, please carry on with your story."

"The movie ended late, so I urged Shannon to go to bed afterwards. I followed about an hour later. As her eyes were closed, I assumed she was down for the night."

"But she wasn't."

"I woke up around three a.m. and noticed she wasn't in bed."

"You became anxious."

"I'm always anxious when she's psychotic. This just magnified it."

"You then searched for her."

"Yes, but she was nowhere in the house."

"So you panicked."

"That's when I smelled the paint fumes from the garage."

"Where you found Shannon."

"With Don's painting! Our son's art that she displayed so proudly!"

"What about it, Charles?"

"She had completely spray-painted over it!"

You forgot to mention with the white, heat resistant kind—an important detail, I added.

"I couldn't believe it! My wife, the woman who frames her kids' work professionally—it made no sense!"

"Why did you do it, Shannon?"

They manipulated him! My tender-hearted son! A child! The one who waits for Mom when no one else does! The one who takes the smallest slice of cake in consideration for others! The one who accepts the chores nobody wants. How dare they! "It's complicated."

My therapist stared firmly in my eyes. "You know what?"

"What?" I retorted.

"I have a sneaking suspicion that your delusions still haunt you."

They aren't delusions! This is real!

"Shannon, I'm not sure I can convince you otherwise. So let's try this. Will you please pretend that Charles and I can't read your thoughts and tell us exactly why you did it?"

You would like that, wouldn't you? Then I'd sound like a fool! "Sure."

No longer a rookie, Charles called my bluff. "*Please*, Shannon."

Sorcery

So, I offered my *verbal* explanation. "I'm a bit of a perfectionist when it comes to decorating."

"That she is!" Charles nodded his head in full agreement.

"Also, I worry constantly about my children's self-esteem."

"Then why did you paint over Don's picture?" our son's father demanded.

"Charles, do you remember the beautiful tree Don painted last week, with the blue leaves?"

"Of course I do."

"Our quiet child, who never draws attention to himself, made a big production."

"He did an amazing job. He was proud."

"A couple of days before that, he confessed that the one I hung was meant to look like the coral reef, but revealed a giant explosion instead. He seemed to regret that I exhibited it on the wall."

"It was a lovely painting, Shannon. Are you suggesting he was ashamed of it?"

"I am proposing that he was uneasy with its translation." *My powers, Charles! I don't understand them! Think of what might have happened—our innocent child would carry that burden!*

"How will you explain this to him, Shannon? How are you going to tell him that you vandalized his masterpiece to 'save his feelings'?"

"I'm not going to say anything."

"He'll notice!"

"I *know* our son. He'll be relieved. Besides, I plan to frame the tree painting as its replacement."

Dr. Russo addressed the most targeted victim of my delusions. "Are you satisfied with her logic, Charles?"

"Do I have a choice?"

Then she looked at me. "Promise us something, Shannon."

"What's that?"

"Next time you rescue someone's dignity, please do it in daylight hours."

If it is only dignity, I will. "You have my word."

Don never mentioned his missing painting on the wall. I suspect that Charles spoke quietly to him about the casualties of mom's sickness.

Chapter Twenty:

Concession

COMBATING THIS CYCLONE of hallucinations and delusions expended every ounce of energy I could muster, and as a consequence, my defenses also waned. My obsession with arriving at Emerald City became a side theme in my journal entries. By this point, reality had escaped me and I no longer understood clearly what my metaphorical destination stood for. I was only certain that once I arrived, everything would be as it should.

Journal
April 5

I feel my gas tank getting low. It's time to stop at a station. Emerald City, are you still there? This map confuses me.

That afternoon, Charles requested that I help pick out new flowers to replace the dead ones in our garden. Believing he was sending me a secret message that Valentino had died, I wept, then consoled myself that maybe I could reform one of the other voices. Were they really so bad? Perhaps they were just misunderstood.

Later, Valentino tapped my shoulder. "I'm still alive—just hiding away for the moment," he revealed.

Relieved, I wanted to send him a message that I had not forgotten him. Yet, how could I do this without anyone catching on? So, I used the method I preferred most, calling him my favorite herb.

Journal
April 6

Today I thought I had lost my favorite herb, and so I watered the garden with my tears. And—voila! It sprang right back up again.

Although it's a bit too spicy for the palates I wish to feed—just knowing it's there consoles me.

My psychologist wanted to find the underlying cause of my psychosis. How did it all begin? Were my delusions the same as last year? How did the two compare?

Today, she would investigate. In order to do this, she showed up as the first group that objected to my delusions—the book club.

"Tell me again about your initial episode. At what point did you become paranoid?"

Who are you today? "Last May, my therapists were a student and her professional mentor. They taped the sessions to review and discuss later. I was aware of this."

"Did the tapes bother you?"

You're someone from Beijing. "Not at first. Then I shared a very personal and private issue with them. Beijing's expat community is quite close and gossip flourishes as it would in any small-town atmosphere. I was squeezed into an even smaller fishbowl, as I was friendly with several people at the international hospital where I was treated."

"And you thought your psychologist disclosed your conversations to your friends?"

"Not exactly. Friends and acquaintances began to make statements that appeared to respond directly to my problem. On top of that, they seemed accusatory. I wondered if anyone was listening to my tapes."

"Did you report this to your psychologist?"

I know who you are! "Jasmine was the student. I liked her a lot. She was sweet and approachable. Dr. Hoi, her mentor, always knew when to jump in and help out, so first, I tested my hunch."

"How did you do that?"

"I deliberately said something offensive about someone I presumed was listening."

"Then you waited for a reaction."

"Exactly, and my friend made a comment the next day that felt like a retort to my statement."

"Were you angry?"

"I was hurt."

The memory of this experience stung. I unfurled my emotions in my journal—in metaphor of course.

Journal
April 7

A park near my home hosts the most impressive garden. Trees, shrubs, flowers, and streams adorn it. She was once my place for speculation. Each path she offered opened my eyes and mind. Her beauty touched my soul. I wore my thoughts and emotions freely. She was my place for meditation.

One day, I accidentally bumped into a hornets' nest. They mistook me for something dangerous and attacked. The multiple stings caused so much pain, I fear returning.

Truly missing her brilliance and depth, I want to visit again. My heart will tell me when.

Chapter Twenty-one:

Accountability

Journal
April 8

This box left on my doorstep wraps itself in layers of riddles.

Hyper-religiosity and grandiosity continued to pester me at church. I could no longer enjoy the music or sermon. Words floated from my preacher's tongue into the air, mingling in concert with the voices beckoning me to become their Jesus. I was also sure that Charles was on the church's side. How could I convince them that I did not want this title? Couldn't they see how unhealthy this was?

Not wishing to offend, I declined their insistent proposal as politely and delicately as possible, and thus my congregation became the metaphorical Lillianville I came to address in my journal.

Journal
April 9

A lovely morning spent in Lillianville! I dropped by for breakfast and enjoyed it so much, I stayed for lunch. The people were warm, friendly, and welcoming. They invited me to attend their spring festival. It was a glorious experience. Delightful sounds entertained my ears as artists played their instruments of wood, metal, and vocal cords. Many people danced and sang along. I did my best to close my eyes and still my body, focusing on the energy surrounding me. The mayor addressed us with an inspiring speech on community involvement. It captivated my heart to be encompassed by people who genuinely want to do their part to make the world a better place.

They tried to get me to stay and even offered me a job. I felt truly honored. As much as I delighted in their company, my heart says to continue to Emerald City. I'm certain that IS my destination.

I'm now on the road again, regenerated and ready to continue this path paved for me.

May we recall Lunacy once again? He was still spinning the hell out of that merry-go-round, and I was holding on for dear life. Believe me. Charles and the kids fretted desperately on the sidelines week after week.

As my mask of sanity was only a costume, madness was broadcast through my eyes. Although I did everything I could to continue

Accountability

the cover in my children's presence, "hiding" this condition was an impossible task. The strain exuded tension all around me, and the burden fell on them.

With one foot in this world and the other on my own planet, Jean received half the attention she was used to getting from Mom. My daughter's needs were not being met to her customary standards. As a cry for her mother's tenderness and recognition, she acted out continually. My jumbled perceptions of her behavior didn't help matters either.

Older and more aware of *why* my conduct had changed, Michael and Don expected the same consideration from their sister. Although they had become quite patient with me, something had to give—and that was their tolerance for Jean. The result was constant squabbling among the siblings.

Trepidation had also taken its toll on Charles. Working full-time in addition to added responsibilities around the house drained his emotional reserves as well. Then there was the stress of dealing with me. Psychosis is not only alarming for the individual experiencing it. It also afflicts the loved ones exposed to it day after day, much like second hand smoke.

Thus, my husband's composure with the kids suffered, as theirs did with one another. It disquieted our home. I could see what was happening, but my state of mind impaired my ability to act accordingly.

Journal
April 10

Today I recognized through the eyes of my children that life is not so easy for them either. They're expected to yield to their parents' moods and inadequacies as much as we are to theirs—perhaps more so.

The delusions and hallucinations continued to manipulate me, informing me that I had offended the religious community with my disregard for their rules. They did not understand why I wouldn't conform, while I, in return, wondered why they had such a problem with me.

What's wrong with my relaxed attitude? Though my lack of ceremony might advertise otherwise, I welcome God's favor as much as anyone does.

Opening my laptop, I continued with an analogy.

Journal
April 11

An interesting building caught my eye today. I recognized it as a restaurant and stopped for lunch to fill my belly. While making my entrance, it became evident that this was a very formal venue. My sweatpants, T-shirt, and ponytail looked a bit out of place compared to the beautifully dressed patrons who filled the room. Nevertheless, I was hungry and requested a table.

Although odd glances and giggles escaped a few folks as they tried not to stare, the waitress offered me a lovely table. I ordered the special and discovered that this establishment was run by a world-renowned chef! Cleaning my plate, I savored each bite.

By the time my tongue licked up the last crumb, no one seemed bothered by my appearance. I think they understood that I appreciated the food as much as they did—even without my pearls.

Accountability

Later, though, I felt contrite about my brash remarks—both telepathic and those addressed to the religious community. The voices in my head confirmed my fear. They interrogated me. "Why do you antagonize theological scholars with your ignorant rebuttals? What makes you more of an expert, Shannon? Have you attended seminary school? Have you studied ancient texts?"

I needed to apologize. Then again, I wanted to make my own wishes clear. I had commanded myself not to become hyper-religious again. It was clearly an unhealthy place to be, and yet the voices infringed, and I believed that the Christian Church had sent them. Yes, I went too far in my retaliation and I wanted to make amends. On the other hand, the church must also recognize my need for personal boundaries.

How could I convey this appropriately? I thought Dr. Sun and a tree would be the perfect platform. So, when she led me to her office the next morning, I was prepared to make my concession.

"How are you, Shannon?" she asked.

Forgive me. "I think I went a bit over my head this week."

"How's that?"

"It's about a very large tree in my backyard."

"How lovely. What kind?"

Time to confess ignorance. "I actually don't know."

"Is the tree sick? Were you trying to treat it?"

"No, it's quite healthy. Unfortunately, it hangs over our pool."

"You don't appreciate the shade?"

"I do! That's why I waited."

"Waited for what?"

"To prune the branches."

"Why?"

"They dropped so many leaves, I couldn't keep them out."

"I see. And that generates issues."

"Exactly!"

"Please tell me that you didn't try to cut them on your own."

"My landscaper offered to do it last week, while working on another project. I declined, thinking I could."

"It wasn't as easy as you thought, huh?"

"A tree that size requires tools and skills I never bothered to acquire."

"So what did you do?"

"I ate a little crow, drove to our landscaper's office, and asked if I could take them up on their offer."

"I'm sure they appreciated your business."

"I certainly valued their expertise."

I never informed Dr. Sun that, in my tangled words, the tree was religion and the pool my spiritual freedom.

I twisted my kaleidoscope once more and what I saw was a book. Not the one I yearned to write, but one I had fallen into: a bizarre fantasy. Had this puzzle not yet revealed the whole picture? Perhaps each chapter offered new insight. Maybe the only escape was to see it through. Was my journal a connection between the novel that imprisoned me and the memoir I wished to compose? I placed this thought in my tablet.

Journal
April 12

Browsing through the library the other day, a book tumbled from the shelf onto my head. Rubbing the sore spot, my eyes fixated on the title. Read Me was all it said. Intrigued, I tucked it under my arm and hastened to the checkout desk. The librarian greeted me with a combination of shock and understanding.

"Where did you get this?"

"It found me—it was a bit painful."

She paused, as if to gather her thoughts before proclaiming her message. "This is an unconventional kind of literature. It pushes buttons you were unaware of and pulls hidden strings in your heart. You might wish to put it down or hide it in the deepest canyon. Instead, I recommend you read it through. When you think you've lost your mind, that's when the mystery begins to unveil."

"Does it have a happy ending?"

"It will pleasantly surprise you."

"It's quite thick. Should I allow a later return date?"

"The book found you. Consider it a gift. After the final word, you'll know what to do—try not to make premature assumptions. There are coils and turns meant for introspection. Allow this, although it will confuse and agitate you.

I accepted the novel, incognizant of how a bundle of paper and words could free my mind and heal my body. As more pages need to be turned, I'm not yet who I want to be.

The hormones of three adolescents, mingled with a psychotic mom and apprehensive dad, continued to unsettle our home, sometimes traumatizing me into flashbacks that cycled over and over in my mind, driving me crazier than I was already. In moments like these, Charles and Marsha collaborated.

Aberration recognized my fragile state and sent my dear friend, Adya, to shine through Dr. Russo's eyes today as she stated gently, "Charles emailed me."

Why am I not surprised?

"He said that something happened over the weekend with your oldest son."

"Yeah, it was upsetting."

"Will you tell me about it?"

"We were all sitting at the dinner table."

"And your son said something."

Shame and fear made my shoulders slump and weakened my neck as I responded. "Michael gathers trivia as a squirrel does nuts, pulling it out to chew on whenever the mood strikes."

"He shared some with you last night."

"Yeah."

"How?"

"It started with my daughter."

"Okay."

"She's studying puberty in class, body changes, and all its attachments."

Marsha could not help but smile. "She's at that age."

"Jean brought up their focus on assertiveness and ways for girls to protect themselves against rape."

Nodding her head in approval, Marsha said, "I'm happy to hear that."

"Me too, but that led to Michael's remark. He pointed out the correlation between male instinct and the origins of rape."

"And that unsettled you."

"It was more *how* he said it."

"How was that?"

"Like a sixteen-year-old asserting his manhood."

"He was a bit cavalier."

"Yeah. He didn't understand how it would affect me."

"But it did."

"Appallingly! You're aware of my sensation of constantly being mentally raped."

"His comment exacerbated it."

"I turned white—had to leave the room."

"Did Charles comfort you?"

"Yes, he must've found me in a fetal position. Afterwards, he spoke with Michael."

"Did your son apologize?"

"He felt awful. He's only a kid. He had no idea how I would react."

I left Marsha's office barely able to walk upright. Flashbacks whirled around me, dodging my every move as I attempted to swat them away. Oh, I hated this screen, playing itself over and over again in my head. How could I make it go away?

Journal
April 13

Maybe if I tell Marsha, they'll go away.

For forty-eight hours, I ruminated about whether or not I should disclose the memories that flashed through my mind. It was humiliating enough to share such disturbing, graphic scenes with the world telepathically, but to describe them aloud? Disgusting!

Then again, that's what the voices told me.

"You aren't transparent enough. Make yourself vulnerable," they said.

But this? Really? Yuck!

Nevertheless, I divulged to my counselor, hoping it would make the images go away. Thank God she showed up as my Mom. Her presence consoled me.

"Remember last week?" I asked.

"The incident with your son?" Marsha recalled.

This is hard. "No, it relates more to the mental rape thing."

"I remember that part too—sounds frightful."

"Well, there's more."

"More?"

"Yeah. I already told you about my flashbacks."

"You only said that you had them. Do they still bother you?"

"Yep, but I need to tell you what they are."

"I'm listening," my psychologist said, her tone softening.

"They're sexual."

"Are they unpleasant?"

I nodded my head vigorously, blurting out before I lost my nerve. "Yes! I hate them. You see, I was molested as a child and it kind of flashes images of that." I gagged.

"Was it by a relative?"

"No."

"Can you tell me about it?"

My stomach churned, threatening regurgitation. I swallowed. "No."

"It's okay," Marsha comforted me. "This probably isn't the best time. Let's get you well first. Then maybe we can address these memories."

Chapter Twenty-two:

Despair

WHEN PSYCHOSIS WRAPPED me up in my own little world, it hindered my ability to see beyond myself. I became narcissistic, believing the world *really did* revolve around me. This feeling of being bigger than life or God-like is a common symptom, called grandiosity. No doubt, every individual reacts to grandiose delusions according to his or her personality. I found it overpowering and felt that I couldn't possibly live up to the expectations the world had of me. Honestly, I didn't really want to.

I was so overwhelmed by this responsibility, along with the belief that the world was watching every move I made and hearing my deepest thoughts—not to mention the screaming voices in my head—that it knocked the breath from me. *How could I possibly withstand such diabolical encroachments?* The weight of it all thrashed through my intestines and heaved the acid in my stomach up my esophagus. My capacity had been breached and the thought of continuing to live like this felt unbearable. I fell to the floor, sobbing, contemplating the relief death might offer.

Before I could even initiate a plan, the voices warned me to consider otherwise. *"Your powers! Don't forget your powers! If all of humanity attaches to your brain, what will happen to the others if you shut down yours? You could very well destroy the world by ending your own life."*

Was this possible? I didn't know. Perhaps they just wanted to keep me here, locked up in my cage of deception. Then again, what if they were right? I didn't want to hurt anyone. At that moment, I lost all hope. For even the choice whether or not to exist had been taken from me. Still, this tragic delusion kept me from killing myself.

Journal
April 15

If I must hold on, God, please at least extend a finger.

As quickly as they pulled me out of the woods, my hallucinations and delusions commenced to badger me again, making my life miserable. They harassed me relentlessly: "The world wants you to be Jesus. Why won't you be Jesus?"

I was so tired of fighting them on this. I could see that a direct discussion would have to take place, and it did, in Dr. Sun's office. For just as Dr. Marsha Russo became the role master—Dr. Sun had transformed into religion's official liaison in my eyes.

Concern crossed my psychiatrist's face as she examined my tightened jaw and colorless cheeks.

"How are you?" she asked.

Tell them to stop placing this crown on my head! I won't wear it!
"Yesterday was difficult. I wanted to die."

"Did something happen?"

"Society keeps pinning this label on my back. I pull it off, only to be stuck with it again."

"The pressure is too much for you?"

They think I'm weak. It takes strength to say 'no'. "It can be overpowering."

"I see. Is the medicine helping?"

You mean religion? "No."

"I'm going to try a different medication. Call me if things don't improve within a week."

This time I'll take it. "Thank you, Dr. Sun."

Laying her hands gently in her lap to soften her demeanor as well as her voice, Dr. Sun spoke tenderly. "You deserve to feel better, Shannon."

However, when it was time to ingest the pink pill, I changed my mind. Three full bottles remain in my medicine cabinet.

Chapter Twenty-three:
Stratagem

I SUPPOSE ONCE one hits rock bottom, there is only one way to go. So, that's where I headed. The night after confronting Dr. Sun, I fell into a deep sleep for the first time in a long while, changing my outlook, and placing a sense of efficacy back into my hands. The next morning, I gave myself a fresh start.

> Journal
> April 16
>
> I'm back on the road to Emerald City. I thought the storm yesterday might delay my trip. It didn't–just offered a much needed rest.
> Some lessons I wish to forget, but then I realize how valuable they are and change my mind.

Although I had no desire to be anyone's savior, I did feel compelled to champion world peace. Therefore, one day when Marsha informed me that I could be anything I wanted, I took her literally. I believed, without a doubt, that my planet was waiting for me to choose a position and that was the real reason for the game they forced me to play. It was my training, to see if I could handle the pressure—and I almost cracked, but didn't.

Thus, I began to study my circumstances from a more analytical point of view. First, I acknowledged the need to quit church, at least until I figured things out. Every time I entered the chapel, the pull to become Jesus stretched my reality into an uncomfortable position and the perplexing language that intertwined between the voices and my pastor's words offered me nothing but anguish.

Admittedly, this decision hurt Charles. As the place that sanctioned our marriage, my husband cherished our weekly attendance. He also revered its values as the foundation on which he wished to build our children's attitudes. I had already held mixed feelings about this before becoming sick, but my delusional angst exacerbated matters.

He accepted my decision reluctantly and took the kids on his own every Sunday, giving me time to consider my next move. I made a "To Do" list:

1. Figure out the truth of my existence.
2. Deal with whatever that truth may be.
3. Take care of my family.
4. Write my book.

Then I pondered the best way to reach these goals. A strategy—I needed a plan of action, but what could that be? What armor could madness not penetrate? *Think, Shannon! Think!* Then it hit me—*physical evidence!* I hopped in my car, drove to the bookstore, made my purchases, and returned home.

Ardently, I inspected seven hundred forty-one pages of definitions. That's what *Webster's New World Dictionary and Thesaurus* offered, and it proved to be quite useful. At first, I dissected word meanings pulled out of this volume. Then I graduated to scientific theories from books, magazines, and the internet. Nonfiction plucked out the fiction bits in my delusions.

*Journal
April 18*

Words to think about:

*Malleable: can be pounded into various shapes without breaking—How has this affected my choices and relationships?
Consistent: in harmony; holding the same principles or practice—What are my principles?
Valid: based on evidence or sound reasoning—Which of my principles are valid and which ones do I need to explore further?
Integrity: honesty, sincerity—Is this how I respond to those I care about?*

Convinced the world had drummed up a system of numbers in its game, I refused to play. If it was my quandary to resolve, I would do it my own way.

*Journal
April 20*

While working out a math problem, it occurred to me that there are many ways to reach a solution. I choose the method that works best for me.

Although our relationship was complicated, Valentino rallied when I had no one else to turn to. Therefore, I called upon him once again—only for a brief time—as I needed his counsel desperately. He understood things would be different this time. I could not afford to be enamored of his charms. Still, he was the only hallucination I truly appreciated, the only one who helped me in times of crisis. And so I beckoned him with a note, placing it strategically in my tablet.

Journal
April 21

He spoke his own language and wore too many colors for their tastes. "Stay away from him!" they shouted.

"He's different. We don't trust him."

His shyness kept him in the shadows, unseen by others.

Then one day, as I made my way through a busy street, I stumbled on a rock, dropping the puzzle left in my care. No one came forward to help—except this gracious man. Stepping out of his comfort zone, he quietly searched and gathered the pieces with me.

That's when I learned that sometimes kindness comes out of a veil people try to keep you from.

I only needed to call and my dear friend, Valentino, ran to my side, ready to assist. I shared with him my list of goals and asked him please to help me with Charles. He agreed and became my confidant and counselor once again.

Stratagem

Charles pulled up a chair beside me at my laptop, biting his nails beneath his furrowed brow as he cast despairing glances my way. "You've distanced yourself from me again. We never talk. You spend all your time on that damn laptop."

Don't pretend to care. "Just trying to record my thoughts. It helps with the whole discerning reality—fantasy thing."

"Am I a fantasy to you, Shannon?"

What about you? How do you feel about me? "No."

"You hesitated."

Do you love me? "Just thinking."

"About what?"

Nod your head if you love me. "About my book."

"Dammit, Shannon! Will you stop thinking about your book for one minute and focus on us!"

So you don't love me—I understand.

Valentino, help.

"I'm going to be patient, Charles. You need that."

"You're speaking nonsense."

"I just mean that I'll focus on your needs more."

This "character" in the ludicrous world I'd fallen into grabbed my chair, physically turning my body toward him, and implored, "Then look at me, Shannon. What I need is for you to talk to me."

Are you biding your time until I say something foolish? Is that what you want? "Okay, then let's talk." *Valentino, will you please mediate?*

Certain that humanity misused my metaphysical endowment, I recruited reformation, support and remained firm in my contentions. First, I needed to approach the stranger who wore my wedding ring, and what better way to do this than with a moderator—Marsha. And so, Charles entered her body.

Marsha showed me the piece of paper. "I received another email from Charles."

Hi, Charles. "There's tension between us."

"Would you like me to read it?"

"Yes, please."

Positioning her glasses, she began.

Hi Marsha,

I'm sorry to bother you, but I'm concerned for Shannon. She says nothing's wrong–that all is okay between us. But she obviously avoids me. When I call her, she rarely answers. Sometimes she doesn't reply for hours.

I try to talk to her about it. She remains evasive, responding with one excuse after the other.

I'm at a loss what to do.

Sincerely,
Charles

I don't trust you! You don't love me! I'm only property to you! "It's all true."

"You can't live like this."

"The feeling that the world is invading your thoughts, using you as a tool—a weapon! Attempting to sway you for its own greedy purposes defiles your happiness. They pillaged life's pleasures when they violated me!"

"Who are you talking about, Shannon?"

Religion, Politics, Big Business. "The world."

"This is fiction."

Do you not understand? If I make it fiction, then my reality ceases to exist. "It doesn't feel that way."

Stratagem

I was going in the wrong direction. My psychologist brought me back.

"We're talking about your husband—not the world. You need to open up to him."

But he's part of it all—the primary schemer. "Right now I struggle to do that with anyone."

"Shannon, consider if the roles were reversed. How would you feel?"

Her words struck a chord. How could I expect my husband—or humanity, for that matter—to show me compassion, if I returned a cold shoulder. I straightened my intertwined fingers, rocking them back and forth in a see-saw motion as I let the thought sink in.

Finally, I replied, "Hurt."

"And you don't believe the same goes for Charles?"

If your words are sincere—perhaps. "I suppose so."

"Then will you try? Reach out to him. He's just standing there waiting, Shannon."

"I'll try."

Marsha was right. I was fighting the man who could help me. I had to figure out a way to trust and work with, instead of against, him. So I returned home, determined to reconnect with the man who said he loved me.

Journal
April 24

Piecing this puzzle together, I can't help but wonder how significant each chunk is. Are the parts or the focal point more relevant? If the background is missing, where does the story take place? Doesn't it set the tone?

Just as the silkworm creates refined elegance in her mundane task, so did Charles and I, simply by collaborating in our own banal exercise. Who would have known how organizing the garage could restore propriety in our home? Possibly, by working productively alongside me, my husband validated that we were indeed on the same team.

He scanned the labeled and neatly stacked containers against the wall and wiped his sweaty brow. "Thanks, babe! We did it."

Placing hands on hips in my own satisfaction, I reviewed all thirty tabs. "We did." *We certainly did.*

"You should finally be able to park your car in here now."

"Yep."

Charles weaved his arms through mine and around my waist, kissing me on my head. "I'm proud of you, partner."

Do you mean it? I couldn't look him in the eye for fear of seeing a lie, but I wanted so much to believe him. "Thanks. We did work well together."

Charles offered a gratifying nod. "We always do."

I surrendered. *You at least like me—I'll give you that.*

I decided to lean on Charles more and say goodbye to my invisible confidant for the last time. I thanked Valentino for his help and he tiptoed out of the room quietly so as not to encroach upon our marriage any longer. With my easy guest gone, I could now attend to the other unwanted hallucinations.

Why did she have to show up as Jean today? I wondered. I could have handled any other possession, but it was definitely my daughter's eyes I saw in Marsha's.

"You're biting your nails, Shannon," she pointed out. "You never bite your nails."

Stratagem

My eyes dropped to my lap. *I'm so ashamed of myself! What kind of mother does that to her child?* "Tomorrow's Don's birthday."

"Are you nervous?"

No! I'm ashamed. "It kind of has me thinking about my daughter's birthday."

"Is her birthday coming up too?"

You aren't listening to me. "I'm talking about her tenth birthday, last July."

Realization dawned on my therapist's face. "That's when you were in the hospital."

"Yeah. I can't stop imagining her celebrating, in my absence." *How could I have done that to my baby girl?*

"You couldn't help being sick, Shannon."

I'm so sorry, Jean! "I can at least be there for my kids. Here I am again—my world flipping in every direction but the right one—on Don's birthday."

Marsha pushed herself forward. "How old will your son be tomorrow?"

"Fourteen."

"Let's try something. I want you to close your eyes."

Eyes shut.

"Imagine Don blowing out fourteen candles. Now envision yourself by his side. Can you see it?"

My jaws relaxed. "Yes."

"Tell me exactly what you see."

"Don is leaning over a vanilla cake smothered in peanut butter fudge frosting. Michael and Jean are singing the 'Happy Birthday' song across the table, while Charles lays his hand on his shoulders and I take pictures."

My psychologist leaned back. "Well, Shannon. If you can see it and you can say it, then you can do it."

Thank you, Jean. Thank you, sweet daughter of mine, for helping and forgiving me. "I feel much better now."

Journal
April 29

Today is Don's birthday. We will commune as a family and make him feel special this evening, and I will not allow my condition to prevent me from celebrating with him.

That evening, I piled the kids in the car and met Charles at The Breakfast Table, Don's favorite restaurant. We enjoyed pancakes and waffles for dinner, along with an embarrassing birthday serenade, and emulated a very mainstream family outing. What is my evidence? The smile that never left the birthday boy's face.

Journal
April 29 continued

Releasing the twine from my ankles, I swim towards a floating object. My upper hand grasps a buoy. Head above water, I now see a lifeboat in the distance. The search team I thought had deserted me is in fact pursuing me earnestly.

Chapter Twenty-four:

Evidence

MARSHA INFORMED ME that she, Dr. Sun, Charles, and my family and friends participated as a unit. Each member played a part, and today this unit would team up with science to confront and intervene on a matter that concerned all of them.

The unit made its challenge in Marsha's voice. "Shannon, I'm going to ask you a question."

"Okay."

Wearing a stern expression, she warned, "I *need you* to be honest with your answer."

What are your intentions? "Of course."

"Are you taking your medication?"

You know I'm not. Why would I?

"Shannon—please reply."

"No."

"Have you told Charles?"

He knows.

"You aren't answering me."

I don't trust him enough yet—to say it aloud.

"Your silence speaks as loud as your words, Shannon."

That's the problem.
"I'll assume the answer is 'no'."
"I haven't told him. I haven't told anyone."
"Not even Dr. Sun?"
"No."
"Why don't you take it, Shannon?"
"It makes me feel bad."
"Dr. Sun works with you, doesn't she?"
"Yes."
"How many times has she switched your medicine?"
"Twice—plus the Latuda I started with."
"Your logic is not yet convincing."
"I research the medicine I take."
"The warnings and side effects bother you."
"Yes!"
"How?"

"It makes me depressed, lethargic, stupid, and fat. Plus, there are serious health risks."

"You could benefit from a little weight gain and all medications present risks."

"But antipsychotics are more toxic than most."

"We're only asking for a year, Shannon."

That's all it takes to kill me. "I have an abnormal ECG. That's how this all started."

"I thought your tests concluded you have a healthy heart."

"Yes, but considering my family history—why would I take a chance on a drug that warns me not to?"

"It specifically points out risks for patients with abnormal ECGs?"

"Yes!"

"What exactly does it say?"

"It says to consult with my physician."

"Have you done this? Have you informed Dr. Sun?"

Evidence

"Well—yeah, but there are other side effects."

"List them for me, Shannon."

You can't stump me. I know what I'm talking about! "Elevated triglycerides, diabetes, liver damage, and—what is it called—when your tongue protrudes involuntarily?"

"Tardive dyskinesia."

"I'm still young. I hope that I'll double this age. Why would I do that to my body?"

My therapist paused. "You know, Shannon, more recent medications, like the ones Dr. Sun prescribes you, hold a much lower risk of all that—including tardive dyskinesia."

"I think I can do this without the medication."

"It's not the easy route."

"I've improved tremendously."

"You've come a long way."

"I want to continue without the meds."

"Then you must tell Charles."

"I will."

"Do you promise?"

"I promise."

"May I call Dr. Sun to inform her? Otherwise, she may never speak to me again."

She already knows. "Sure."

Why did science phone in my last session with Marsha? They were trying to tell me something. Perhaps it was my next clue. I needed to explore other avenues to unwrap the riddles around my box.

Journal
April 30

I consider myself the artistic type. However, I'm often attracted to people with science backgrounds and find it fascinating when they explain these principles to me in a way I can understand.

I began to read about Einstein, the atom, and his theory of relativity, convinced it would all help me solve this puzzle, needing to understand if it were possible scientifically to emit brain waves telepathically. If I could prove its impossibility, my most dreaded delusion would cease to exist, possibly returning the joy of life to me.

That said, my philosophical mind could not transform into a purely methodical thinker overnight.

> *Journal*
> *April 30 continued*
>
> *On a map, north points up and south points down. West points left and east points right. However, our planet actually rotates in space, where there is no direction. When I say, "My world has turned upside down," has it really?*

Could it be that my reality was merely a different way of looking at things. If so, did that make it backwards? Perhaps not.

> *Journal*
> *April 30 continued*
>
> *What I like about both my psychologist and psychiatrist is that they each provide tools, offer their professional counsel, and then encourage me to select the most suitable options, while doing my own research.*

I would try to receive as much advice as I could. Ultimately, however, it was up to me to decide how to make my decisions and approach my problems.

Evidence

The three superpowers—big business, politics, and religion—continued to pound on my door. Their ardent demands provoked me. I simply could not accept such an invasive display in good conscience. Perhaps if I addressed my concerns verbally to Marsha with these strings attached, humanity would finally *get it*.

Bonnie possessed Marsha, appreciating that I needed a sensible soul on my side today.

"At the end of the session last week, you mentioned your humiliation. Will you explain?"

How can I illustrate this? "Imagine society as a puppeteer."

"Okay."

"He seized me in my sleep, injected my arm with a sedative, and then he commenced to place a false mask on my face, boring hooks into every joint, before threading his wires of manipulation and deeming me his Shannonette."

"You feel controlled."

"That reveals one third of the picture."

"There's more?"

"Positioning me before the camera, he counterfeited a song and dance, while narrating a concoction entitled, 'Shannon's Life'."

"So you're also on display."

"To exacerbate matters, this puppeteer is in fact Dr. Jekyll!"

"Oh dear."

"When his alter ego works the puppet, he hijacks orbiting satellites and displays this absurdity on every electronic device on earth."

"As a joke?"

"As a brainwashing tool."

"So, you're not simply concerned for yourself."

"This is an international predicament!"

My therapist stopped for a minute, allowing us both to digest the load I had thrown on the table. Then she allowed her eyes to survey my entire body. "You often show up in exercise clothes, Shannon."

"My health is important to me."

"You look fit. Do you do strength training?"

I grinned. "Yes."

"I've heard that Dr. Jekyll was all brain and no brawn."

"I know where you're going."

"Where, Shannon? Tell me."

"You think I can take him. You want me to yank the stick right out of his hand."

"If you can say it and see it—"

"I can do it."

Marsha's words echoed what I had said all along. I had control of my own life. If I didn't like the picture it portrayed, write it down in my own words. Allow the world to *read* my voice.

Somehow, her validation stamped an "official" hallmark on my work. Now, more than ever, my book's significance gravitated to the number on the scale it rested upon, and when I uncovered my eyes, *infinity* replaced unbefitting numbers.

And so, I cut the strings and consummated the plan.

Journal
May 1

I will no longer sit through this farce of a contingency. I have a book to write. These feet were made for walking and they'll be walking right out of here!

Then I unlocked the safe that guarded my hidden emotions. Two months of obscured darkness deterred them from stampeding. Instead, they tiptoed out cautiously, a few at a time.

Journal
May 2

I'm going to be brave.

Officially, I reversed roles with my delusions. Instead of them controlling me, I now began to control them, using one to combat another. Thus, in my journal, my book and my hand collaborated to write me out of this predicament.

It was time to take a positive but logical look at how I would perceive life, humanity, and myself.

Journal
May 5

I desire not to insult my intelligence by limiting myself to effortless tasks. Instead, I choose to believe in myself! In return, my faith in those around me also increases.

My friends and family had waited patiently by the sidelines, rooting me on, but my symptoms prevented me from accepting their support. Finally, capable of a semi-rational conversation, I received a Skype call from Adya.
"Hey you!"
I peeked through the screen to study my friend. "You still aren't showing. Any morning sickness?"
Pulling her shirt tight, she flattened it against her belly. "A little baby bump, which is good, as I can't seem to keep my breakfast down."

I smiled. "You look adorable!"

We chatted about her pregnancy and the kids for awhile. Then Adya broached the obvious subject. "Charles has been updating me, but I'd like to hear from you. How are you?"

Still trying to figure things out. "Much better—but a ways to go."

"What's the worst part?"

I didn't hesitate to reply. "Being watched by the world."

Adya's eyes crinkled. "Do you still believe that?"

"I'm working on it."

"That must stink!"

"Tell me about it. Michael and I actually had this discussion last night."

"He knows?"

I shook my head. "Not sure. I posed it as a 'What if this was possible' question."

"Being watched by the world? I can see your oldest sinking his teeth into a discussion like that."

"Yeah, it's right up his alley."

"So—?"

"So what?"

"How did you respond, if you didn't want him to know about your delusion."

"I attached it to my symptoms last year."

"And?"

"I listed the pros and cons of how the delusion affected me."

"There were benefits?"

"Yep. It made me more aware of my own morality and how my words and actions affect others."

"Really?"

"Sure. When you think people are observing your every move, you feel like a role model. That, in itself, changes the way you behave."

"What's the worst part?"

Evidence

"Thinking that all of humanity can read my mind strips me of my freedom of thought."

"A nightmare!"

"You said it, sister!"

Chapter Twenty-five:

Emerald City

HUMANITY CLOAKED MY skull with a new layer each day and, gradually, the voices dissipated. As my extended security system complicated daytime attempts, deception shifted to evening heists—sneaking into my dreams. However, I had studied these hallucinations in the daylight, reviewing their calculated moves over and over in my papers. I was a force to be reckoned with.

Fraudulent mind games were no match for me. Refusing to waste time on such deviousness, I simply addressed them and moved on to matters that are more important.

Journal
May 7

Last night I dreamed I was taken by force to an extremist group influenced by hate and violence. Immediately recognizing their intentions, I stated emphatically, "This is not me!"

Shifting my eyes in every direction, I searched for an escape.

Thankfully, it was only a dream.
Here I am consoling myself.

Above all, I insisted on keeping a positive attitude.

This morning, much to my dismay, I opened the file to my book and many pages of hard work were missing! I glared at the roadblock with panic and frustration. Then Helen Keller grabbed my hand, signing, "When one door of happiness closes, another opens, but often we look so long at the closed door that we do not see the one that has been opened for us."

Instead of fretting over lost efforts, I will twist my kaleidoscope once more and examine the design it presents.

The week commemorating my lost brother approached, triggering memories of my fall off the wrong side of the bed the previous year, when I attempted desperately to retrieve him from his unjust incarceration in Hell. This year I was inclined to celebrate the two still with me.

Journal
May 7 continued

I have three brothers.
Austin—the first I lost eight years ago this month. Thirteen months apart, we shared our entire childhood together. We played and quarreled like most siblings.

I certainly taunted him and pushed his buttons, as any little sister would, but our memories, both good and bad, cemented a history I have not shared with any other.

Glen–the second, born on Austin's eighth birthday, has a gentle disposition. He annoyed us sometimes, like a typical little brother. Mostly, he entertained and amused us. The way he looked up to and admired his big brother and sister gave us a confidence we would not have enjoyed otherwise.

Jason–the third arrived almost a decade after me. His feisty energy and birth order produced a toughness that only comes from surviving three older, very spirited siblings. I lacked patience with him as a teenager and berated him in my frustrations, as I now witness my own teenage sons do with their younger sister. He visited me sometimes in the summers after I married. Now I respect him as a father who cares for his family and a man who works hard to overcome life's obstacles.

All three of these men brush the background against which I am featured. Our indifference to phone chatter leaves long spans without conversation, but absence does not bother me, for Certainty assures me that time and space will never erase our mutual love for and loyalty to one another.

When I was sick last summer, Glen and Jason each visited me in the hospital several times. They were two of the few people with whom I felt safe. I will label that as "physical evidence."

Then, however, a flashback to an event that occurred in my church three months after my brother's death haunted me. The preacher began a fire-and-brimstone sermon with a coffin carried down the aisle by six men, as if in a funeral procession. "Heed!" he demanded. "If you do not save your loved ones from the depths of Hell now, then soon it will be too late!"

Sweat and anguish swept my body, as I remained trapped in the middle of the congregation. Panic froze me into the pew, while my ears attended to the single most traumatic event of the year after Austin's own funeral. This tirade not only replayed my brother's memorial, but also insisted that by not saving him, I had crumpled his soul—throwing it into the pit of hell. For my brother was an atheist.

Swiftly, I grabbed my tablet and washed this deception away with a breath of fresh air.

Journal
May 8

The Receiver

"Chikma (Hello), Aiyana."

Itanale and Omba peeped their heads through the old widow's doorway. It was their usual time to visit. Mama's encouragement was not necessary. They genuinely enjoyed the company of the grandmotherly figure.

Because Aiyana was barren and unable to have children of her own, she delighted in their company and relished their youthfulness. The children raced to her home each day after their lessons and chores, to assist her with her work. Later, Aiyana served grape dumplings and entertained them with various tales.

As Aiyana approached the end of her time on this earth, she searched for a gift—something to give Itanale and Omba before she left. One evening while nibbling at her corn and squash, it came to her. "I will share with them my father's secret story."

She did not make this decision lightly, for it was only meant to be passed down through the bloodline. However, Aiyana's circumstances had changed from previous generations. Being an only child, she understood with clarity that her ancient gift would die with her if she chose to follow such a rule. The beauty of this treasure outweighed tradition.

Brother and sister listened intently as their dear companion and mentor made her offer. Although the siblings shared an altruistic view of life instilled by their parents, their approaches differed.

Itanale accepted graciously. Such an honor was humbling and she understood how it warmed the widow's heart to name her inheritors.

Omba, on the other hand, felt that accepting such a legacy would invalidate their relationship. He did not wish to water down his genuine efforts by reaping a reward at the end. He declined modestly.

Understanding good intentions from both children, Aiyana devised a plan. When Itanale stayed behind the following day to receive her story, the young and old contrived a solution.

That night and each night thereafter, Itanale pretended to sleep, biding her time until her brother slipped into slumber. Then, she tiptoed quietly to his side and whispered Aiyana's words in his ear. Itanale repeated this until the day their friend's spirit transcended.

Upon her departure, they sneaked into her home one last time. As they drank in the memories, Omba spoke. "A dream has come to me with the stars for some time now, in black and white. In this hut, Aiyana's aura paints it with color."

"Yes."

> "You too?"
>
> "Her words sculpted it for me. She understood that you needed a different way. You see, my brother, she could not only give to me. Her story was meant for both of us."
>
> A sense of peace and contentment fell over the two souls as they understood Aiyana's wish had come true.

The anniversary of my brother's death caused me to reflect on that year of grief. Part of my religious heritage instilled the idea that we must accept a gift—the gift of the Savior—to avoid dire circumstances once our heart stops beating. The idea is beautiful, because grace is simply an unearned gift.

However, Austin would suffer under this concept.

Morality and this traditional theory once conflicted in my mind.

Appeased, I finally chose to believe that such a selfless person would not be punished on a technicality.

Journal
May 9

> Marsha mentioned the movie *A Beautiful Mind*, the biography of John Forbes Nash, Jr., a schizophrenic mathematical genius and Nobel Peace Prize winner. Although he contributed much to society, he seemed lonely.
>
> This condition stimulates my mind on a plane not otherwise attainable. It also isolates me.
>
> My objective is to step back into my social skin without releasing this gift–the vision of my kaleidoscope. If it can be done, it'll be worth the bumpy ride.

Emerald City

Charles' phone buzzed. It was time to get up. Instead, he slid his body next to mine, swaddling me with his arms just as he did before I was sick. It had been a long time coming.

He pressed firmly against me. The warmth from his chest penetrated through my back. I welcomed the heat. For the past two months, our bodies had separated themselves between the invisible force field I installed in our bed. Shattering it was today's triumph.

"You feel good." His voice was husky.

I smiled. "Mmm—so do you."

"Tomorrow, we see Marsha."

"Yep."

"Is there anything you should tell me before we go in?"

"I think she just wants to hear your perspective on my progress."

Caressing my arm, he buzzed in my ear. "You're doing well right now."

The familiar texture of his masculine touch invigorated me. My skin tingled and I knew what my husband wanted, as the same desire also stirred inside me. Nevertheless, my sensuality needed more time—more coaxing to thaw out...and the anxiety...why did my husband's stroking fingers both arouse and dishearten me? I wanted him. He wanted me. Why wasn't I ready? *Take your time*, I consoled myself. *You've already accomplished a lot this morning.* Finally recognizing that my body would not cooperate fully with its titillation, I flipped over, kissing the forehead of my redirected lover. "Thanks, baby. And *now*, you need to get dressed for work. Moaning, he released me reluctantly and hopped into what must have been a cold shower.

I continued to lie there, following this gorgeous man with my eyes—still wanting him. Shame flushed from my neck up to my cheeks. Depriving Charles was unfair—after all, it was his spousal privilege as well as mine. We were regaining the trust and intimacy that my apparitions had stolen from us. I knew without doubt that it was time to re-consummate our marriage. Recognizing our need for release, I resolved to take the plunge that night and held myself accountable by putting the decision in writing.

Journal
May 10

I'm naturally a romantic person. Psychosis stripped that from me. Tonight, I'm going to watch a passionate movie with my husband boldly and relish in the deliciousness of it!

But the fire it ignited burned my lover's fingers, as fear of being watched by the world inhibited me from having sex with Charles until we were hidden safely under the covers of our bed, doors closed, and away from all technology, all the while pleading over and over in my head, "*Please no one listen! Please no one listen!*" which led to a lackluster experience compared to our once amorous relationship. Pent-up sexual frustration boiled well above my husband's eyeballs. His accompaniment to my next session with Marsha offered him an opportunity to voice his own discontent.

She wore our old marriage counselor's mask this time, a most appropriate choice.

I couldn't withhold my joy at seeing his spirit in her eyes. *Brian! I'm so glad you're here!*

"Hi, Charles. It's nice to see you again," my therapist remarked as he faced Charles.

"Shannon seems to be progressing well from what I can see. What is your take?"

"She's much better than she was two weeks ago."

"But she's still not quite herself?"

"Not yet."

"What still concerns you?"

"Electronics."

"What about them?"

"She refuses to be intimate with me around them—not even in front of the television."

"Is this true, Shannon?"

It's this "whole world watching" thing. I just can't stand the idea of it, in the bedroom—or in any intimate moment, for that matter—it makes me feel like a porn star. "Yeah, it's a barrier."

"This morning when I checked on her in the shower, she screamed just because I had my phone in my hand."

"I didn't scream, Charles, and your phone happens to have a camera attached."

"She ordered me to leave."

"Did you, Shannon?"

"I can explain."

"Please do. It helps us understand where you're coming from."

"Before my relapse, I took my laptop to my bathroom to use as a radio while I showered and dressed in the morning. One of my initial delusions was that someone tinkered with my computer and broadcast me dancing naked in my bathroom."

"How could they do that?"

"I assumed through Skype."

"And now you associate all electronics with this experience?"

"Especially those with a camera."

"What will it take to get past this?"

I need to be one hundred percent sure that I'm not being observed by others. "Time, and feeling safe."

My husband and I left Marsha's office with a little more empathy for one another, welding another layer to our connection.

Journal
May 11

A delightful weekend awaits:
- *Charles and I spend Friday together.*
- *Michael applies for his driver's permit.*
- *I celebrate Mother's Day with my family and my very cool friend, Ling, who is visiting from Beijing.*

Sunday morning, Charles' and the kids' muffled voices, along with the chinking of dishes, woke me up behind my closed bedroom door. Nevertheless, I appreciated their good intentions, and waited patiently for someone to retrieve me. Jean led me to the breakfast table, where two elaborate place settings adorned with gifts and homemade cards were prepared for Ling and me.

I admired the presentation, and then regarded my husband with adoring eyes. *This man loves me without doubt.*

We ate our breakfast, read sweet notes from the children, and opened our presents. Then Charles, the man I accused of degrading one of my heroes nine weeks prior, presented me with an envelope. Opening it, I found two tickets to the Broadway musical, *Evita*, playing at the downtown Houston Theater.

My husband beamed. "I thought you and Ling could enjoy a girls' day—go to the show—then, maybe dinner afterwards."

I shot up from my seat and jumped upon this beautiful man's body, entwining him with my arms and legs, and then planted a gargantuan kiss on his mouth. *Let the world watch,* I screamed mentally. *This man is my angel.*

The boys excused themselves politely after breakfast and returned to bed, so the rest of us made our way into the living room, where my husband plopped himself into his favorite chair, and we three girls found cozy positions on our leather sectional, where we hung out and got lost in chatter for the next couple of hours. Charles asked about Vincent, so Ling brought him up to date on her husband, followed by the details of her son's graduation and his career plans; she finished with the latest reports from Beijing. We, in turn, relayed how the kids were doing in school and the particulars of Charles' new job, along with life in Houston. Our easy camaraderie launched one hour into the next in a flash, and before long, it was time for Ling and me to get ready.

After grabbing the tickets and my purse, Ling and I headed out the door, already giggling and full of energy—and that's when I noticed it. In all the morning's excitement, I didn't apprehend the absence of intrusive language. I didn't recognize my lack of concern for the delusions that had been haunting me for more than ten weeks now. I reached over and hugged the precious woman standing next me.

"Thank you for coming to see me. You couldn't have picked a better time."

She hugged my neck. "I'm so glad you are up to it."

Ling and I rushed through lunch, but not so fast as to abandon conversation. And since it was our first moment alone, she finally asked the question disturbing her thoughts since she had arrived. "How are you—*really*?"

As one does with a trusted companion. I confided. "It's been hell. But things are much better now."

Demonstrating her caring and inquisitive nature, she investigated further."I've done a bit of research—trying to understand what you're going through. You can't determine reality from your delusions. Is that right?"

"It's the spur in my heel and it has tortured me."

Confusion wrote itself all over Ling's face. "You seem to be with me now—very present and lucid."

I smiled at this stabilizing force in front of me. "Funny thing—I've been slowly making my way to Emerald City. Your arrival, my friend, seems to have placed me on the fast track of that last stretch."

Blinking her eyes and shaking her head, she stated the obvious. "That made absolutely no sense to me."

I slapped my forehead to push out the laugh. "Sorry. One of my delusions has been this compelling force to reach a symbolic place I've called 'Emerald City' for the past few months. I finally understand what it means."

"And what is that?"

"Clarity. I was desperately seeking my way back to it—a little like Dorothy, I suppose."

"Are you there?"

"I think I am, thanks to you."

"Me? I haven't done anything."

"You're here. I think that was the last stitch I needed to sew this baby up."

Ling giggled. "Well, you're still talking kind of funny. But I think I get the point. Thanks for thinking so much of me."

I leaned over for one more embrace. "Thank *you*."

We swallowed our last bite and headed to the theater.

As usual, Charles did not spare expense and we found our seats in the center of the fourth row from the stage. This time, I enjoyed the performance as any spectator—merely a portrayal of a legend—no hidden meanings.

Ling and I then headed to a local coffee shop and jabbered a bit more, like any two girlfriends whose words never run dry. We reminisced and laughed until my phone rang.

"No rush. But, where are you at?" It was my husband.

I looked at my phone and saw that five o'clock had already approached. Although I enjoyed every second with this gal, I also wanted to share a Mother's Day dinner with my family. We headed home recognizing that fate could not have brought a more perfect individual with whom to celebrate, for Ling always had a way of making me relax and forget my worries; and at the moment I needed it most desperately, she did just that. As on every other occasion I have spent with this vivacious woman, we had so much fun that day.

That night, while lying in my husband's arms, I replayed the events of the day. It had been the most pleasant *and* normal one I had enjoyed in awhile. Contemplating the reasons for this difference, I recalled a discussion Ling and I had that afternoon.

We were discussing the challenges of living in a big city and maneuvering ourselves effectively within its complicated road system. As a self-confessed "directionally challenged" person, I explained my "no fail" escape plan when I get lost.

Three major expressways run north-south in Houston; one crosses them on an east-west perpendicular angle, and small and large loops each circle the city. As long as I understand this basic design, I simply find the closest beltway that will take me to the path leading home.

Likewise, the complicated infrastructure that mapped pathways through my consciousness underwent massive reconstruction as it continued to adapt to my psychotic existence. Fortunately, certain freeways remained constant (i.e., my husband's love for me, my love for my children, and the support of family and friends). When disorientation prevented me from functioning joyfully and productively, I made my way to those familiar routes. This safety net allowed me the freedom to explore my delusions and learn from them. Now that I had found those paths, I could return home, back to stability.

When one is out of her head, it appears to the beholder to be the other way around. Insanity finally left the mouths he spoke from, and I welcomed Clarity's voice as it returned its sweet harmony. Marsha and I could now become acquainted, as my relapse had permitted very little time alone before she played the Role Master.

Now, finally, I conversed with Dr. Marsha Russo *as* Dr. Marsha Russo.

"You look great! I've missed your smile," she acknowledged.

Grinning, I greeted the true spirit behind the face. "Thanks, me too."

"How are you?"

"Fantastic!"

"I'm so glad—it's been a tough ride."

"But I did it—we did it."

"You weathered the storm."

"I'd like to thank him."

"Who?"

"The storm."

"Why is that?"

"Because he sired my baby."

"Your baby?"

"My book."

"Then he'll have a *lot* of character."

"She's a girl," I corrected.

"What did you name her?"

"*Twisting My Kaleidoscope*."

Unrestrained laughter erupted from my therapist's belly. "Quite appropriate!"

"Thanks."

"So—no more delusions?"

"A bit of residue."

"How much?"

"About five to ten percent."

"Any triggers?"

"Certain statements—it's more like the evening after a movie."

"What do you mean?"

"Have you ever watched a horror film?"

"I have in the past—I usually avoid them."

"Why?"

"Because they tap my shoulder at every dark corner afterwards."

"Certain comments become those corners for me."

"How long before you're convinced it was just a movie?"

"It depends on my baby."

"Your book?"

"I'm still nursing her."

"Oh."

"I tend to hold onto five or ten pounds until my children are weaned."

"When will that be?"

"When I hand her over to the publisher."

Removing the massive weight of the rock from my shoulders, I set it properly where it belonged, beside my final piece of evidence.

Journal
May 15

> **Omnipotent:** Having unlimited power or authority–all-powerful. **Proof to myself that I am not an omnipotent being:** If I were, I would understand how to rid the world of atrocities such as injustice, hatred, violence, terror, hopelessness, sickness, and hunger, without relinquishing love, individuality, passion, and pleasure.
>
> How I wish I could gift such a thing to my brothers and sisters, as I assume many of them would grant the same. Alas, I do not know how.
>
> Perhaps, if I give more than I take, in some small way, my contribution to society will make a difference.

Grandiosity made her exit. What a relief it was to be free from such an overwhelming sense of responsibility.

Contemporary theories, such as quantum physics applied to philosophy, posit that our perceived consciousness is reality. Like most ideologies I have examined, I find some truth in it. My psychotic encounter imprinted a memory as vivid to me as any harrowing experience in a person's life. For that reason, it was my reality.

Likewise, concrete evidence provides the stability necessary to function productively and contentedly in society. Retracing my steps to those reliable passages supplied a lifeline out of the turbulent waters of psychosis.

Free at last, I merely toyed with metaphor for sentimental reasons, as I had indeed reached my destination.

Journal
May 17

Imagine my surprise when I stepped in the Emerald City Welcome Center this morning, greeted by Charles and the kids!

"How?" was all my mouth would form.

Charles wrapped his arms around me. "Your stubborn insistence forbade my physical presence, but I remained with you all the way, through your stories on the phone, and in my dreams at night."

"We arrived yesterday, Mom," Jean piped up.

Don grinned. "All your chatter piqued our interest. We wanted to see what the fuss was about."

"And we missed you—a little," Michael added sheepishly.

"You drove?"

"No!" They all laughed.

"We flew. You're the only one crazy enough to do that."

I suppose they're right.

When Professor Aberration imposed again, she demanded I complete my "homework" before graduating. The first time, Latuda stamped my papers, allowing an early release. Possibly, she charged me with cheating. "If you had studied as you should," she scolded, "you could answer the test questions and be on your merry way."

Momentarily excusing myself from Charles and the kids, I approached Dr. A. at the Welcome Center help desk. She presented me with my final exam:

1. **Who am I?** I am a wife, mother, daughter, sister, a friend, a teacher, student, writer, individual, and a member of humankind. Above all, I am someone who gives and receives love.
2. **Why am I like this?** Perhaps because my fluid existence prohibits precise shaping, I'm meant to moisten the parched ground beneath my feet.
3. **Where am I going?** Emerald City, of course! If by good fortune they publish these pages, I entertain visions of book signings and inspirational visits to psychiatric hospitals.
4. **What gift did the riddled-wrapped box present?** My family.

Turning in my paper, self-satisfaction, admixed with uncertainty about Professor Aberration's response, churned within me. I hovered as she traced my answers with eyes, red pen, and indeterminate mumbles. At the end, she merely wrote, "PASS."

"Am I finished? May I go?" I pleaded.

"You are clear—for now, Ms. Love. However, my course must sometimes be refreshed. Do you understand?"

Consternation flushed cold sweat over my body. "Again?"

My teacher's steely expression melted into a tender smile as she glanced at the four people waiting for me in the corner. "Only if needed. Don't worry about what you haven't yet written. Enjoy the chapter you're in. I see it contains some lovable characters who wish to share it with you."

Her wisdom penetrated my pores, suffusing my entirety. Rehabilitated, anxiety's haunts evacuated my body as I accepted my diploma, flipped my tassel, and made my way into the arms of my beloved.

Sheer determination fueled my tank as I ventured on my quest for sanity. Those who love me would have commissioned a less tumultuous excursion, but then there would be no tale at the end of my tail—and now I wag it happily at you, as it says goodbye, for I will join my family and revel in this city I have worked so hard to reach.

Note From Author

After suffering a psychotic break in midlife, I berated myself for the anguish and shame I placed on myself and family. Fortunately, professional and emotional support clasped their hands around me, thwarting a hard blow of my skull against the ground. My circumstances differed drastically from most who suffer similar episodes.

"How?" you ask.

A bag of good fortune. Allow me parade these treasures:

1. **Unconditional love**—My husband, children, parents, siblings, friends, and family called, visited, prayed, listened, defended, and sympathized. I have bragged many times of my "good taste in people." It's true. Even during paranoia and isolation, they loved me through it and forgave my irrational thoughts in the end.
2. **Commercial and monetary advantages**—Confessing inequity, I admit the benefits of privilege. My husband's employer values and endorses work-life balance. Between

their financial backing and sentiment we accessed the top quality care and time away from work necessary for recovery.
3. **Exemplary mental health efforts**—In a two-year window, I tallied the aid of four psychiatrists and eleven psychologists! Each of them offered unique tools for my shed. I utilized them all at one point or another.
4. **Thirst for knowledge**—Never satisfied with only the words of experts, I also clutched their hands. An avid reader, I chewed and swallowed print from various books and websites. Advocating diverse philosophies and models, these experts offered wisdom and I filtered and applied what worked for me.
5. **The head of a pig**—I truly am *a stubborn woman.* As I once expressed to a friend, "I talk to God all the time—just mostly we argue." Anyone who talks back to Mr. Almighty has no issues quarreling with Professor Aberration.
6. **My Tablet**—The most effective medication was my laptop. Placing my dispute in print made it official. If I did not wish for a delusion to be true, I simply wrote my contract. That made it so.

Unfortunately our planet does not grant such concession to the majority, offering little or no relief to most who suffer from mental illness.

At the apex of life's roller coaster, we wave our hands in jubilation. But when the track inverts us, instinct screams "Hold on for dear life!" If the lens of delusion rests upon our nose, simultaneously excitement transforms into hysteria. Consider this before criticizing eyes you cannot see through.

Instead, when you pass a homeless person in the parks or streets, reach into your soul and throw her a gem. Perhaps that's all she needs to carry her one or two steps forward. As television broadcasts violent acts of a lunatic, imagine what might have been if the felon

Note From Author

had received sufficient mental health care prior. When tabloids slander public figures for bizarre behavior, acknowledge the human suffering behind the Hollywood mask.

Do I beg you to be superhuman and rescue the world? Certainly not! I just proved its impossibility. Simply open your heart, delight in life's joys, and offer compassion when your mind wants to judge. Are your ears weary from my constant babbling? Please accept my apologies. Like others who survived wars such as genocide, natural disasters, injustice, cancer, and rape, I too wear my badge of honor with pride and passion.

And at that, I bid you adieu, for I have a world to see and a new chapter just itching to be written.

Epilogue

Oh how I wish I could inform you now, how I rode off into the sunset and never suffered from another psychotic break. But that would be dishonest. Since my intentions are to provide a truly authentic description, I will move into what happened next.

A few months after my second recovery, I chose to ignore my still-fragile state and travel extensively. It was an unwise choice. For my symptoms returned once again.

Distraught and depleted of energy, I contacted both my psychologist and psychiatrist. Marsha and I agreed that my battle might be better fought in the hospital this time. And Dr. Sun arranged for me to stay in a small, intimate facility, known for its warm, supportive atmosphere. I remained there for ten days.

After departing the rest home, Dr. Sun worked with me to concoct the most effective medicinal cocktail. A few months later we settled on two pills: an antipsychotic and an antidepressant. In my eyes, this amazing woman worked a miracle. For the first time in two years, I did not have to choose between lunacy and depression. Because every antipsychotic I tried induced an uncomfortable sense of desolation in my psyche, I simply could not bear taking one without a secondary capsule to combat its distressing side effect. My psychiatrist, a wise woman, realized that I would eventually drop the tablet that kept me sane, unless she offered me a solution.

My stance on medicine: it's not fun, but sometimes necessary. As a nonprofessional, I recommend that every individual suffering from mental illness work with a psychiatrist and psychologist she trusts to decide what works best for her. Meanwhile, I'll cross my fingers in hopes for better medical options in the near future.

Will I suffer from another break? I'm too optimistic to say, "certainly" and too realistic to say "no." Life throws wrenches into everyone's existence one way or another. Psychosis just happens to be mine. Lucky for me, my incredible support system will be standing there—ready to catch me if I fall.

Disclaimer

As I mentioned in my acknowledgments, my support system was monumental, leaving me with a problem. Who would become characters in my book? I trimmed the selection down to the ones with which you became familiar. However, some of the scenes actually took place with individuals not highlighted—relevant conversations worth including. Hence I merged words of my other beloveds into the mouths of those featured.

I also fabricated a few scenes as a way to better convey my psychotic experiences. Thoughts, delusions, and hallucinations that I struggled with, but did not necessarily share with anyone, needed to be displayed in a way that you, the reader, could visualize them. So, in order to provide you with a more comprehensive experience, I took creative liberties.

One scene, my brother's car accident, happened at a much earlier time (a couple of years prior). I chose to place it in that particular spot as a replacement of another equally upsetting event, and as a means to protect the privacy of other characters.

You could say, this book is ninety percent nonfiction and ten percent creative invention. That being said, I tried to be as truthful as possible about my psychotic experience, itself.

CPSIA information can be obtained
at www.ICGtesting.com
Printed in the USA
FSOW03n1545050515
6933FS